Education in a
Free Society

*The Hoover Institution
gratefully acknowledges
the support of*

JOANNE AND JOHAN BLOKKER

on this project.

Education in a Free Society

Edited by
Tibor R. Machan

HOOVER INSTITUTION PRESS

Stanford University   Stanford, California

www.hoover.org

Hoover Institution Press Publication No. 475

First printing, 2000
06 05 04 03 02 01 00   9 8 7 6 5 4 3 2 1

Manufactured in the United States of America
The paper used in this publication meets the minimum requirements
of American National Standard for Information Sciences—Permanence
of Paper for Printed Library Materials, ANSI Z39.48–1984. ∞

Library of Congress Cataloging-in-Publication Data
Education in a free society / edited by Tibor R. Machan
    p.   cm.
Includes bibliographical references and index.
ISBN 0-8179-9832-2 (alk. paper)
    1. Public schools—Social aspects—United States. 2. School choice—
United States. 3. Education and state—United States. 4. Education,
Compulsory—United States. I. Machan, Tibor R.
LC191.4 .E4247 2000
                                                    99-055365
                                                        CIP

CONTENTS

ACKNOWLEDGMENTS

I WISH to express my gratitude to the Hoover Institution on War, Revolution and Peace and its director, John Raisian, for generously supporting the publication of this work. Heartfelt thanks also go to Joanne and Johan Blokker for their generous support of my scholarly projects at the Hoover Institution. I also wish to thank the contributing authors for their cooperation, patience, and conscientiousness throughout the entire publishing process. Last but not least I wish to thank Pat Baker, Ann Wood, and Marshall Blanchard of the Hoover Institution Press for their extensive and very helpful assistance with the completion of this volume.

CONTRIBUTORS

J. ROGER LEE is a retired professor of philosophy who has written extensively in the field of epistemology, political theory, and prison reform.

CAROL B. LOW is a clinical psychologist who has published work on various topics in the psychology of learning.

TIBOR R. MACHAN teaches at the Argyros School of Business and Economics, Chapman University, and is a research fellow at the Hoover Institution. He has written extensively in ethics and political theory.

SHELDON RICHMAN is editor of *The Freeman* and has written books and articles on public education and other public policy subjects while a fellow at the Institute of Humane States and the Cato Institute.

EDWIN G. WEST is a professor of economics at Carleton University, Ottawa, Canada, and author of several books on the history and role of education in North America.

Public Education
and Its Pitfalls

Tibor R. Machan

AN ASPECT OF the fully free society that leaves many people shaking their heads is the rejection of public education. Yet compulsory, tax-funded schooling is not consistent with the principles of a radically, fully free society. Some even insist that public schools are actually coercive, a forceful violation of individual rights.

They maintain this for two reasons: Not only are elementary and secondary schools funded by taxes, which are a relic of feudal states in which monarchs took what people produced as payment for the privilege of working in the realm the monarchs owned, but, even more repulsive, students are forced to attend, never mind what their parents or they themselves want to do about their education. It is like military conscription, which since Richard Nixon's time has become nearly voluntary. In a free country both of these are anomalies. One need only recall the Declaration of Independence in which it is held that everyone has the right to life, liberty, and the pursuit of happiness and that governments are instituted to secure these rights. How can this be consistent with public schooling?

Despite what seems to be an obviously anomalous system, citizens have become accustomed to public schools. They believe that public education is responsible for the prosperity of the United States of

America, even though this is highly questionable. What seems to be a much better candidate for the cause of that prosperity is the system of legal protection given to our basic rights, including freedom of production and trade. Nevertheless, many seem to feel comfortable with and depend on public education not just as a school for their kids but as a kind of surrogate home, a kind of child-care service.

Yet just because something has become part of one's life doesn't mean there couldn't be a basic flaw in it. After all, some of us have bad habits such as smoking or driving too fast that may be difficult to overcome. In American society slavery was an evil to which many southern whites were accustomed, indeed on which they economically depended. Thus white southerners fought a Civil War that had as part of its focus the question of slavery. They were wrong.

It could be the same with public education. Slavery and conscripting young people to public schooling are not identical in their moral gravity, but they arguably share some fundamental features, namely, the massive use of governmental power to support the extreme regimentation of the lives millions of human individuals.

This book posits that those concerned with public affairs need to explore why public education is an anathema to those who see themselves as fully consistent champions of human liberty. This may seem unthinkable to some, but there are reasons for serious worries about public schools.

For one, as already noted, government in the American political tradition is supposed to secure our basic rights to life, liberty, and the pursuit of happiness. This does not include embarking on such projects as fostering the arts, healing the sick, manufacturing cars, growing food, or educating our children. Furthermore, government schooling also involves a highly dubious "one size fits all" approach to education, which is problematic if children require different upbringings.

Also, confiscating money from all property-owning citizens to fund education for those with children is morally repugnant in a genuine free society. That, however, isn't the main focus of this volume, although most of the contributors assume that free people should not be forced to pay for things; free people's money should be voluntarily spent, not coerced by a jail term if they refuse to pay.

The primary concern in this book is whether human individuality is compatible with coercive public education. A free society should be the best polity for accommodating our essential human individuality. People aren't all the same, even as children. The mostly one size fits all approach to education is, thus, arguably misguided and ultimately damaging to learning. When it comes to exercise, nutrition, clothing, or even medicine, we see that human individuality determines what is right for or of value to us. Why not in education?

Incidentally, this is not relativism but the recognition that what is truly right for people is intimately connected with who they are, their individual personalities, as well as their human nature. Yes, some very general needs, including educational ones, are shared by all children. Yet this is akin to us all needing clothing and nourishment without us all wearing the same garments or eating the same foods. Similarly, we all require education but in a great variety of shapes and forms, based on who we are as individuals.

Americans, especially, with their insistence on doing things their own way, ought to have a clear appreciation of this part of social life. Even in places on the globe where uniformity is the dominant way of social life, it is often widely resisted. (In Communist China, for instance, where at one time everyone was made to dress the same way, people retained some measure of distinctiveness by varying the fabric of their uniformly blue pajamas.)

One reason so many millions of people have found and still find America an attractive place in which to live and raise children is that they see it as a land of opportunity in which they can live a great variety of kinds of lives, not one kind alone. Consider how and what people worship, their religious convictions and affiliations. In America choice is of the utmost importance, and no one should be forced to go against his or her beliefs.

Why should that not hold for how parents educate their children? After all, how one worships may affect the fate of one's everlasting soul, so if people needed government regimentation in that significant area of their life, surely it would qualify more than primary and secondary education.

Some initial points will illustrate the plausibility of resisting the one size fits all approach in education. School systems often have various ideas as to how pupils should be educated—for example, year-round schooling, uniforms for students, the same starting time for all students, teaching evolution versus creationism, drug-testing and search policies, and so forth. Are these proposals all equally good for each student?

In modern societies many students live with a divorced parent during their summer vacations, yet the school administrators often don't take that into account, even though a child might thus be kept from spending important time with one of his or her parents. Some students may indeed benefit from conformity in dress. For others, though, that might not at all be suitable. Yet administrators are willing to contemplate imposing uniforms on all. Finally, every child must start schooling at the same age, start at the same hour in the morning, and so on. Is this really the best way to educate everyone?

What about the more substantive issue of what children are to be taught? Should everyone be forced to learn evolutionary theory or creationism or Spanish or French or the piano or even mathematics at the same time and pace, given the enormous differences among human beings? Using the one size fits all approach will cause most of them to resist the educational experience, dread it, and treat it as their enemy.

By the time many students leave public school—and often private ones, as well, which must conform to state standards—they see education not as enlightenment but as imprisonment. As a college professor I often see students enrolling with great reluctance, mainly only to satisfy their parents or in the belief that without college they will not be able to get a job. Few look toward the college experience with enthusiasm, mainly because of what their elementary and secondary schooling taught them: It is all a chore.

Many things would need to be dealt with if elementary and secondary education were all private, removed—as is religion, which cannot be said to be less important—from the authority of the state. How would children of negligent or extremely poor parents get educated? What about schools that would not be suitable for those who planned to attend them? Other issues are sure to arise in dealing with such a system.

None of these, we shall see, are insurmountably difficult. None, I would maintain, would result in the violence done to children that is done at public schools—not because the teachers or even administrators are corrupt but because the system rests on false premises about human nature.

CHAPTER ONE

Limits on Universal Education

J. Roger Lee

HUMAN SURVIVAL AND FUNCTIONING

Human beings are living creatures. Living creatures undergo processes to stay in existence. For humans, the processes are of two different kinds, physical or psychological.

Physically, life can be sustained in most cases if basic food, clothing, and shelter needs are met. The human organism must be protected from germs, acquire basic nutrients, and be situated in an acceptable environment for living, usually a shelter.

Human psychological functioning for survival is more complex. Plants function and live without a psychological dimension of functioning. Animals have limited, built-in, psychological propensities. These propensities yield activity when they are cued by perceptions or when they instinctively discharge, or when both triggers of action work together.

Humans must function, psychologically, in extremely complicated ways. Further, many complicated functions must be learned by humans before they can be put to the work they have to do. In the first decades of life children learn, largely from other people, how to do necessary human psychological functioning. Much of this learned functioning they will then have to use for the rest of their lives.

There are many psychological needs that are not yet met when human infants are born. Humans have a need for factual knowledge about many things—germs, nutrients, clothing, shelter—if they are to survive. They also need to know about relations of causation if they are to orient to a changing world. They need to know about communication and socialization if they are to orient to their social world. And they have to know principles of correct reasoning so they may arrange their stored knowledge in orderly, useful, informative ways.

Psychologically, humans need more than just factual knowledge. They have a need for realistic, psychological self-acceptance, because humans have to act in the world. Human functioning involves seeing a necessity of action in a situation and then confidently undertaking effective action. Human action requires that an acting human have a sense of his own competence and of his worthiness for acting.

Humans have a need for emotional intelligence. They have to be able to identify their emotional reactions to any particular situation and weigh the human importance of those reactions. They have to sense aspects of the importance of the situation to themselves through these emotions and through other knowledge-based evaluations. And they have to do these two things simultaneously. Humans must sense both the constraints and the resources that their emotional reactions to situations provide for their acting wisely and well in those situations.

Humans have to coordinate their factual knowledge with their feelings and abilities, and then act intelligently. Fundamentally, humans have to act intelligently to meet the bare needs of the organism for mere survival. At a richer level of human need, humans have to coordinate their knowledge, feelings, and action capabilities to meet more complex psychological needs that present themselves to a self-aware, self-accepting organism. As humans develop they should find nobility, beauty, and joy in acting in the right way, at the right time, with the right people, to the right extent—as an intelligent human should. To have this joy is a proper end of intelligent human action. Experiencing this joy is the fulfillment of a human need that is as much worth pursuing as is staying alive itself.

CHILDREN AND HUMAN NEEDS
AT THE START OF LIFE

If children had to fend for themselves from the moment of birth onward they would fail. Physically they are frail and have to be protected from external dangers by clothing, cleanliness and, shelter. Further, they have to be fed and washed and kept at a proper temperature and must be monitored for illnesses or accidental harms that they could not deal with on their own.

Psychologically, infants lack all the sophisticated functioning a human must have to function well in the world. They have none of the factual knowledge that a human must use to survive. They have no developed emotional intelligence. Their emotions offer only the charms or torments of instantaneous emotional reactions to their environment. They know nothing about coordinating knowledge, emotional reactions, and action capability to select action intelligently. They have never experienced the joy of full adult human functioning. Left to their own devices they would clearly fail to survive.

It is a characteristic of animals generally that adults have to meet the physical and psychological needs of their offspring for a long time before the offspring can likely be able to fend for themselves. Until the offspring have developed into young adults, the older adults will have to attend to their basic food, clothing, and shelter needs, sustaining their lives. Adults must provide them with proper nutrition. Adult animals must shelter their offspring from hostile weather, germs, and other predators.

Adult animals also have to train their offspring, giving them assistance in developing their potential physical capacities for action in the world. Offspring have to be brought to an awareness of their physical action capabilities, and have to acquire a sense of control over those capabilities. Animals train their offspring toward that end.

Adult animals also train their offspring to awareness of, development of, and coordination of their psychological capacities. This training is limited in nonhuman animals as are those very psychological capacities. It is on this topic that the tales of human and non-human animals' rearing of their offspring diverge. Humans have to do much more in this domain, and for a longer span of time, than do other animals of other species. Simply because the psychological needs for human action are so much more complex and diverse than are those of other species, so too must humans' efforts to develop those capacities and to coordinate their use in the young be more complex and diverse.

Psychologically the life of the infant when born is at its starting point. There may be psychological tendencies that formed in the womb, but there is no sense of self in the newborn infant. An infant's sense of herself does not come until there has been a good bit of mother-child interaction.

The infant child has no factual knowledge, and therefore no intelligence about the use of knowledge and feeling in action selection. It has some emotional reactions but these are uncoordinated and are not limited by any emotional intelligence of the sort that will be acquired in later years. The newborn child does not have the psychological wherewithal to function for survival. Such wherewithal must be developed through the intervention of adults in the life of the child.

Education in this context is directed activity of children guided by caregiving adults, which activity develops the children's physical and psychological capacities for functioning in the world as required by the nature of life.

EDUCATION IS FOR VIRTUE

Thinkers as diverse as John Locke,[1] Immanuel Kant,[2] John Dewey,[3] and Horace Mann[4] all embrace an ideal: that the core goal of human education is the child's development of a virtuous character.

One's character is a set of tendencies one has. For example, one may be easy to anger, or one may be generous. These may be tendencies involving thought (being inquisitive or rattlebrained or quick-witted). They can be tendencies involving feelings (being defensive or self-pitying or empathic). Many characteristics are tendencies to act in certain ways (being vigorous, generous, or quick-acting). Each of these would be characteristics of the person spoken about. A person's character is the full set of all their characteristic tendencies. More exactly, one's character is the psychological network of dispositional propensities to think, feel, and act in fairly regular ways in situations calling for thought or feeling or action.

1. "It is virtue then, direct virtue, which is the hard and valuable part to be aimed at in education; and not a forward pertness, or any little arts of shifting. All other considerations and accomplishments should give way and be postponed to this." John Locke, *Some Thoughts Concerning Education.* 1693, §70. (http://www.socsci.kun.nl/ped/whp/histeduc/locke.)

2. At least that part of education (moral) that transcended practice and discipline and involved the weighing of general principles (maxims) focused on virtue. "Moral culture must be based upon maxims, not upon discipline. The first endeavor in moral education is to establish a character. Character consists in the readiness to act according to maxims. . . . He can therefore become morally good only through virtues. . . . Everything in education depends upon one thing: that good principles be established and be made intelligible and acceptable to children." Immanuel Kant, *The Educational Theory of Immanuel Kant*, E. F. Buchner, trans., ed. (Philadelphia: J. B. Lippincott Co., 1904), paragraphs 77, 78, 102, 103; pp. 185, 186, 210, 211.

3. It is a commonplace of educational theory that the establishing of character is a comprehensive aim of school instruction and discipline. John Dewey, *Democracy and Education.* 1916, Chapter 26, §1. (http://www.ilt.columbia.edu/academic/texts/dewey/d_e/chapter26.html.)

4. Horace Mann, *Lectures on Education* (New York: Arno Press and New York Times, 1969), pp. 16–17.

To say that the goal of education is to develop a virtuous character, then, is to say that certain tendencies of thought, feeling, and action are to be developed—virtuous ones, or virtues. Virtues are characteristics that make us tend to think excellently, or feel excellently, or act excellently. The opposite of a virtue is a vice. Vices are characteristic tendencies to think, feel, and act wretchedly. A person whose character predominantly is made up of vices is said to have a vicious character.

The Greek word that we translate as "virtue" is "*aretê*," a word that conveys more of our sense of the word "excellence." Virtues or excellences of being human are constitutive of the person who has them and are exercised in actions of that person. The same can be said for the vices that are shameful and debased ways of being human.

One acquires the virtues through the training offered by parents, teachers, and others who care for one. Hopefully, these people have practical wisdom to impart. One acquires virtues through training by having one's actions and feelings habituated to patterns that conform to the virtues. A child's rational faculty will be trained habitually to be sensitive to aspects of situations calling for action, feeling, and thought. The psyche of the child must be trained to the excellences of (1) seeing the relevant features of situations, (2) making judgments that track what is fine, noble, or beautiful in actions and feelings relative to the situation, and (3) selecting what action to take in order to be an excellent human.

Someone who has honed all these skills and tendencies for action will characteristically seek to discern and undertake fine and noble actions and goals of action. Such a person would be repelled by the prospect of actions and goals that are base or ignoble. Taken together, these excellences of thought about situations and about what we should do is called "practical reason." The Greeks called it *phronêsis*.

To say that virtue is the goal of education, as so many people do, is to say that education is to train a child to develop characteristic ways of thinking, feeling, and acting that realize human excellence—

that realize human fineness, nobility, and beauty. A person who develops the virtues and acts in terms of them, the tradition maintains, will live a full life, will live well, and act well. Such a person will have command of his functions and will use them to select the right act, at the right time, about the right things, in the right way, to the right extent, with the right people for the sake of realizing what is fine and noble.

It is only such people who can avail themselves of the good things in life, getting all the good possible out of them. Put negatively, someone who is without virtue, or worse yet is vicious, will not be able to integrate the good things of life into her life in a way that would be good for her. Frequently such a person will attempt to use some good thing and find that the good thing doesn't seem to be good for her or, worse, is even harmful.[5]

In light of this description of the ideal of virtue, it is hardly surprising that the educational community holds that we should educate children for virtue. After all, we all want the most excellent, best possible lives for our children.

VIRTUES AND CRAFTS

In the theory of human excellence it is wise to draw a distinction between, on the one hand, virtues or excellences that are constitutive of the excellence of a person and, on the other hand, whatever crafts or arts that a person uses to make things. Virtues are the acquired skills of being an excellent person. Crafts or arts (*technê*) are skills that are focused on producing things.

In themselves, crafts and their exercise are neither good nor bad aspects of a person's life. Using a craft is not, in itself, an excellence or a virtue. The exercise of a craft will be good or bad solely depending

---

5. A full working out of such a theory of virtue as human excellence can be found in Aristotle's *Nicomachean Ethics* and his *Eudemian Ethics*.

on the worth of the object produced, in the situation in which it is produced. On the other hand a virtue is good in and of itself, as a human excellence.

This distinction between crafts and virtues, though important to an account of human excellence, is very much less important to a theory of education. Not only do we want to educate our children to develop into excellent beings, but we also want them to be able to produce the things they need in order to live fully and well. We want to educate them in productive skills not only for their own good but, in justice, to produce and give as good as they get in social interaction. As John Dewey phrased it: "There is an old saying to the effect that it is not enough for a man to be good; he must be good for something. The something for which a man must be good is capacity to live as a social member so that what he gets from living with others balances with what he contributes."[6]

Education, therefore, is both for developing virtues and for developing productive crafts in students. Humans have to be trained in both if they are to flourish fully and well. Virtues and crafts share a common denominator: They are both skills. Each is a disciplined way of thinking or feeling or acting relative to some goal, either the goal of producing objects or the goal of realizing human excellence.

SKILLS: UNIFORMITY AND UNIQUENESS

Virtues and crafts are the same for everyone. To be brave is to feel appropriate fear, think of what should be done, and then do what should be done, even in the face of fear. That's what it is for me, that's what it is for you, that's what it was for Sergeant York, for Elizabeth I, and for every other brave person; so too with the other virtues and crafts: They all are defined the same for everyone.

On the other hand, a virtue such as bravery manifests itself dif-

6. Dewey, *Democracy and Education*, Chapter 26, §4.

ferently in different people and in different situations. What concrete thoughts, feelings, and actions a virtue guides an individual to will differ from individual to individual and from situation to situation. For example, consider three different people witnessing the early signs of a street crime. In that situation, the thoughts entertained, the feelings had, and the actions undertaken by (1) a brave sedentary middle-aged academic, (2) a brave soldier on leave, and (3) a brave 88-year-old woman using a walker will be very different from one to the other of these people, all of whom are brave in so acting.

It's the same with crafts. Cooking is cooking—you, I, or anyone might take some food, wash it, trim it, and prepare it. We'd all be cooking. But the details of the exercise of the craft of cooking will differ greatly among a highly trained chef preparing a banquet, a tired teacher throwing something together for a quick bite to eat, and a working short-order cook. The prepared foods that are produced through these three different exercises of the craft of cooking will be different, too. And the criteria of evaluating the worth of the prepared food generated by these three will also differ.

Early virtue theorists knew this well and insisted on it. Consider, for example, Aristotle writing about the virtue of temperance. That is the virtue that guides a person to eat an amount of food that is less than too much but more than too little—guiding the person to eat a correct amount between those two extremes. Aristotle insists that, whether an amount of food is moderate or extreme, the right amount will vary from person to person. Taking the extremely contrasting cases of the legendary strongman Milo of Crotona and of a youth just beginning to undergo strength training, he wrote:

Suppose that 10 lb. of food is a large ration for anybody and 2 lb. a small one: It does not follow that a trainer will prescribe 6 lb., for perhaps even this will be a large ration, or a small one, for the particular athlete who is to receive it; it is a small ration for a Milo but a large one for a man just beginning to go in for athletics. . . . In the same way then an expert in any art avoids excess and deficiency, and seeks and adopts the mean—the mean that is not of the thing but relative to us.[7]

And in the domain of crafts, professional tool-buyers have long known to buy different tools for their firm's carpenters than would those same buyers buy to use on rare occasions in their own homes. A good hammer for a homeowner to have to hand for occasional need is not likely to be a good hammer for a professional carpenter to use all the time in his work.

LIMITS ON UNIVERSAL TRAINING
IN VIRTUES AND CRAFTS

To be brave, a person need not have the training and knowledge of a professional soldier. To be prudent, a person need not have the training and knowledge of an efficiency expert. To be able to read and write, one need not have the training in or knowledge of language that a professor of linguistics should have. To do the occasional plumbing repair that falls to a homeowner does not require that the homeowner have the skills possessed by a working plumber who has mastered his craft.

We must educate our children in the skills that are virtues and crafts. The education received by everyone, however, is and ought to be but a small percentage of the education received by one who will come to be an expert in any domain of human endeavor.

Thomas Jefferson, an early American advocate of universal free public education, advocated limiting the content of the universal part

---

7. Aristotle, *Nicomachean Ethics*, 1106b1–6. Machine-readable text. From *Aristotle in 23 Volumes*, Vol. 19, translated by H. Rackham (Cambridge, Mass.: Harvard University Press; London: William Heinemann Ltd., 1934). The Perseus Project. (http://www.perseus.tufts.edu/cgi-bin/text?lookup=aristot.+nic.+eth.+1106b#fn1106b.)

of education. Just after the adoption of the Declaration of Independence, he proposed such a scheme for his state, Virginia. The proposal was many-tiered, with the universal part of free public education being limited to a small, core content. This common core, he proposed, should be taught to all children in three primary-school years. These children would receive lessons in reading, writing, and the most elementary arithmetic, and would be brought to an acquaintance with Greek, Roman, English, and American history. Only one male[8] student from a group of schools in a district would then be publicly supported for one further year in a district grammar school on the basis of being "of the best and most promising genius and disposition" and "whose parents are too poor to give them farther education." Anyone else may attend the grammar schools and continue education further, but at private expense. After one year only two-thirds of the supported grammar-school students were to be offered public support for another year, after which all but the one most accomplished publicly supported student would be dropped from support. The one remaining supported grammar-school student who is outstanding in genius and disposition would be publicly supported for only four further years of education.[9]

Jefferson's proposal quickly sketched here was written for a very different world from that of the early twenty-first century. Much can

8. Thomas Jefferson and John Locke lived in a social milieu and time in which they, like the vast majority of their contemporaries, thought that only male children should receive an education. That they believed this is regrettable, of course, and I flag their having done so by using the male-gender-specific bits of language they used when I report their views. Jefferson, to some credit, did hold that both boys and girls should receive three years of universal education at a below-grammar-school level that is spoken of here. Locke sometimes argued for a relaxation of the traditional curriculum in boys' education by pointing to how well women functioned, even though they had had no education in the matter at hand.

9. Thomas Jefferson, "A Bill for the More General Diffusion of Knowledge," *Public Papers*, pp. 365–373. Electronic Text Center, University of Virginia Library. (http://etext.lib.virginia.edu/etcbin/browse-mixed-new?id=JefPapr&tag=public& images=images/modeng&data=/texts/english/modeng/parsed.)

be said against it, but he clearly has two things right. The first was the insight that very few children will benefit from advanced scholarship, given the lives they would then have been expected to live. The second thing right in Jefferson's proposal is the suggestion that what all students need to learn to lead virtuous, productive lives is a very small number of commonly understood skills—in his proposal, reading, writing, elementary arithmetic, and an elementary appreciation of social and political history.

Perhaps Jefferson, who was influenced so much by the thinking of John Locke, had taken up Locke's quite extreme view that very few children should receive instruction in grammar. Jefferson did place grammatical instruction in the nonuniversal domain of the grammar schools.

It is worth looking at Locke's proposal to limit grammatical instruction to all but a few students. The proposal first shocks us, living as we do in an information age. Second, Locke explicitly follows the principle that universal education should be given only if it will be universally useful, meeting a real need of each of the universe of the universally educated. Were he to have been right about the facts he deploys, his case would have been convincing.

About learning a language, Locke claimed that the "the most expedite, proper, and natural" way is the one by which we originally learned our first language, through conversation. What we pick up over time in conversation with others gives us sufficient command of a language to do what most people want to do with one. According to Locke what most people want to do with a language is to use it, "for the ordinary intercourse of society, and communication of thoughts in common life, without any farther design." No one, Locke assured us, "learned his mother tongue by rules." If we had never had instruction in grammatical rules we could speak well enough to make ourselves understood, understand others' speech, and get on using speech in social intercourse. Were these the only skills the vast run of people needed to function well, there would be no reason to inflict grammatical analysis on the whole lot of students.

Locke did think that a number of people did have reason to study and master the very useful skill of grammatical analysis. The study of the grammar of one's own language, Locke held, is important only relative to the aims of the few people of his day who were members of the very socially restricted class of gentlemen. These men (and he was one of them) should study rhetoric and grammar. For such men, Locke agrees, it is not enough to be understood. These men have the further needs of speaking, and of being observed to speak, with a studied elegance, and "without shocking the ears" of those they address, avoiding "solecisms and offensive irregularities." Speaking with such elegance requires mastery of grammar. However it, like haute couture and other modes of elegance, Locke took to be not a need of any but a few people.

Even a typical gentlemen, Locke thought, had no reason to study the grammar of Latin (unless one were a scholar or wanted to "make speeches, and write dispatches in it") or of other foreign languages. Foreign languages might well be learned but "[i]f his use of it be only to understand some books written in it, without a critical knowledge of the tongue itself, reading alone . . . will attain this end, without charging the mind with the multiplied rules and intricacies of grammar."[10]

Locke's time and social setting is not our own and the literal adoption of his policy as he states it is not defended here. There is, however, a core of truth in his attitude to language instruction: Instruction in skill x and the extent of that instruction should be limited by the use to which the student is expected to put skill x. *Arguendo*, for most people in Locke's time, language was only used for the purposes he indicated and grammatical ineptitude would not, or most rarely would, impede a speaker's realizing those purposes. If that

10. Locke, *Thoughts Concerning Education*, §168.

history is right, there would be no reason for Locke's contemporaries to teach grammar to the vast bulk of their children.

Locke and Jefferson both knew people, and took themselves to be people, who should have and did pursue grammatical skill. Locke was a medical doctor and a politician traveling in Court circles. He also made impressive and influential contributions to scholarship in his free time. Jefferson was a lawyer and a successful statesman. The professional and intellectual activities of these men required a clarity of thought and analysis demanding the most exact grammatical awareness. Their education would have, and should have, differed in content from that of a man whose everyday job was loading beer kegs onto wagons and whose leisure-time pursuits were restricted to imbibing beer and a bit of barroom sociability.

Even if there is a common core curriculum that should be taught to every student, the young Jefferson, Locke, and the young beer-keg teamster, there will be much further education that would be undertaken by gifted and willing scholars, like Locke and Jefferson, but not undertaken by everyone.

It follows from the nature of virtues and of crafts that one learns them without learning the details of their application. One learns to be just and considerate but does not learn whether justice will demand policy j in future situation k. One learns to be just and considerate but only lawyers and jurists even seem to approach knowledge of the details of justice and considerateness for all cases. The humble expressions of puzzlement and of being at a loss to see any ideal path to take, that are frequently made by leading jurists, are exemplary on this point.

The early mathematics teachers of the child Isaac Newton, or even those who later taught him more advanced mathematics, could have had no knowledge of the mathematics he would later invent (calculus) to pursue the details of a physical theory that they could not have anticipated. Those teachers trained Newton in the skill of mathematics, but they could not have trained him in the details of the applications he would make of those skills.

Those teachers who in the 1950s guided me to acquire the few mathematical skills I use in my basically nonmathematical life could have had no appreciation of the fact that for most real-life calculations I would press buttons on a calculator. And the many dreary, directed hours I spent drilling in the finer points of penmanship now seem to have been in excess, too. My teachers did not and probably could not anticipate that I would live in an age of word processing and e-mail and official records kept not by hand but in typed documents or in computers. It was good for me to learn to write with a pen. Back in the late 1940s, however, my teachers did not and cannot have had an accurate idea of the ways their students would use their hard-won skills of pen-wielding.

We want our children to be educated to lead just, considerate, prudent, brave, productive lives in the future. We want them to have all these virtues and we train them to have them. We do not, however, know details of the issues about which they will have to be just, temperate, or brave. We cannot tell them now all the details they will have to figure out for themselves in being just, temperate, and brave.

We are in the same position in educating our children for craft skills. We do not know the modes of productivity that will be open to our children in the future. All we can do is train them in some basic skills and hope that they will use, modify and, in some cases, abandon those skills wisely in the future.

If we adopt the thesis that we should universally educate all children of a community to virtue and craft, the very nature of the goals of imparting these skills demands that the part of education all students learn uniformly should be small and elementary. It is good that all students who are to have future lives together should learn the same basic arithmetic. It would be chaos if different schools taught systems that encompassed different multiplication tables. It is useful that they all learn the same language, to speak it, write it, and read it. It is good that they all learn facts about causation and the sciences that discern it and about some technologies that use it. It is also good that students come to have a broad, common awareness of the nature of human goodness, and then of the nature of their society, its institutions, and their ability to use or change it.

The last paragraph only begins to indicate a core minimum skill and knowledge base in which every child uniformly should be educated to acquire virtues and crafts. Some of the skills we should teach are crafts and virtues; others are simple coordination facilitators that teach students who are being educated to live and work with each other in a community how to function together. These students all must speak the same language, use the same arithmetic—base ten, not base three. They must all have some shared elements in their theories of human ideals and of the nature of their common society if they are to take responsibility for it in their future.

I now turn to other considerations that limit the scope of what should be uniformly taught to all students in a community.

DIFFERENCES LIMIT UNIVERSAL EDUCATION

Every child is equal in citizenship, in rights, and in legal standing in the community. At the same time, every child is markedly different from every other child. They differ from each other in initial character, intelligence, emotional orientation, physique, stamina, interests, and more. There are limits on universal uniformity in education imposed by the fact that children are different from one another.

I use another text from John Locke to guide exploration of this kind of limit. Locke envisioned education as being primarily for developing virtue. He advocated educating children at home, to avoid the corrupting influence that other children at a school might provide. The family, he thought, should conduct the child's training in virtue, usually with the help of a governor in their employ. The education provided, from family to family, would be as diverse as families differ from each other in character and in conceptions of the good.[11]

Locke further held that the education of individual children should be nonuniform from child to child in another way, even in the same family. This new difference in educational activity is required because education in virtue has to be fitted to the character that a child initially presents. Education for virtue must take that initial temperament and, working with it, shaping it along its natural tendencies, working on only those features that can be used for shaping those tendencies for excellence:

> He, therefore, that is about children, should well study their natures and aptitudes, and see, by often trials, what turn they easily take, and what becomes them; observe what their native stock is, how it may be improved, and what it is fit for: he should consider what they want, whether they be capable of having it wrought into them by industry, and incorporated there by practice.[12]

The educator, having acquainted himself with those details concerning his charge, then has to use an adult's superior judgment as to which of the child's tendencies and proclivities to encourage, and in what direction, in shaping the child's character. The educator must decide what is possible given the child's natural temper, and then "whether it be worth while to endeavour it." One may have great aspirations for a child's development and see how he can be shaped for it, but the path might be too arduous to be realistically attainable

---

11. The French Enlightenment mathematician and social theorist, Condorcet, cited this reason, that in religion, politics, and morality "opinions are not shared by all citizens," as a reason for excluding those topics from universal education. A fuller statement of Condorcet's position is provided below. Marie-Jean-Antoine-Nicholas of Caritat, Marquis de Condorcet, *On Public Instruction, First Memorandum: The Nature and Purpose of Public Education,* Part 3, §3. (http://ishi.lib.berkeley.edu/hist280/research/condorcet/pages/instruction_english.html.)

12. Locke, *Thoughts Concerning Education,* §66.

without harming the child in other important ways. The result of the educator's initial inventory of a child's traits may lead to a realistic moderation of goals. "In many cases, all that we can do, or should aim at, is, to make the best of what nature has given, to prevent the vices and faults to which such a constitution is most inclined, and give it all the advantages it is capable of."

To attempt to build on what is not present in the child to support it would be idle. To attempt to force the child to assume propensities and tendencies that are foreign to it "will be but labour in vain." If we succeeded in making the child adopt foreign traits and tendencies that are incompatible with the child's natural spirit, "what is so plastered on, will at best sit but untowardly and have always hanging to it the ungracefulness of constraint and affectation."[13] Such a result, of course, would be an achievement (soi-disant) in moral education devoutly *not* to be wished for.

Although the virtues (and crafts) are the same for all people, educational content and activity used to instill the virtues in each child has to be selected to access the unique abilities, limitations, spirit, and personality of each child in the way Locke indicated. In this sense differences in the pre-educational states of children mandate nonuniformity of education.[14]

---

13. Ibid.

14. Other thinkers echo Locke's analysis of this issue. For example, two and a half centuries after Locke, the American philosopher and theorist of education, John Dewey, reiterated the claim that children come to education, each with a different temperament. Then, citing Jean-Jacques Rousseau with approval, Dewey warned us not to "indiscriminately employ children of different bents on the same exercises; . . ." The danger of this practice, Dewey and Rousseau cautioned, is that doing this will destroy children's unique gifts, leaving only "a dull uniformity." Further, Rousseau and Dewey urged, any gains we might attain at the cost of undermining the child's personality will be but a "short-lived and illusory brilliance" that will "die away, while the natural abilities we have crushed do not revive." Dewey, *Democracy and Education*, Chapter 9, §1.

DEMOCRACY, FREEDOM, AND UNIVERSALITY

All education is the disciplining of one person by another. In educating a child, adults restrict the child's freedom. It is permissible for parents, teachers, and other adult caregivers to restrict and discipline children. These adults' relative maturity gives them a developed ability to deploy the skill of reasoning about values, deciding what is valuable for a child's development. Children lack this skill when adults start to educate them and cannot reasonably exercise their freedom concerning values. Adults who are focused on the child's well-being and development have to do it for them.

As elaborated above, the purpose of education is to develop adult-level skills about values (virtues and crafts) while the child is growing into a young adult. The purpose of education is to train the developing student to be able to exercise her freedom with practical wisdom. There is a theoretical tension here that must be addressed.

There is a tension between our willingness to restrict a student's freedom and the purpose we seek in doing it—to enable the student eventually to undertake free action. Immanuel Kant addressed this tension, writing:

> One of the greatest problems in education is, How can subjection to lawful constraint be combined with the ability to make use of one's freedom? . . . I ought to accustom my pupil to tolerate a restraint upon his freedom, and at the same time to make good use of his freedom. Without this, all is mere mechanism, and he who is released from education does not know how to make use of his freedom.[15]

Bereft of practical wisdom, a child's freedom is mere willfulness. Nature demands that successful human action be in line with its laws, laws that are themselves indifferent to the well-being of any

15. Kant, *Educational Theory*, paragraph 29, p. 131.

person. We cannot act against those laws—we have not the power, we have not the freedom. Human freedom amounts to our finding what the laws of nature let us do and then in acting in concert with those laws to advance our ends.

Even though humans can and do use these laws of nature for their own good, a person—child or adult—who undertakes mere willful unplanned behavior will have defaulted on a human's responsibility. That person will have defaulted on the responsibility to coordinate action with the causal nexus that is nature. Educating humans for freedom is training them in the skills of using the laws of nature to realize excellence or to produce good things. As such, education has to inform the child, making him capable of practical reasoning and of free, human action.

Humans prepare their children to deal wisely with nature. We do this, not by letting nature bring willful children up short; that would be too dangerous a correction in most cases. Instead, humans substitute adults' disciplining and sometimes punishing children as a correction to unreasoning, youthful willfulness. We do this to train the child to more sensible ways of thinking, feeling, and acting. Disciplining or punishing children in education must always be subordinate to the justifying end of contributing to their developing their practical reason, virtues, or skills of craft.

Care must be taken against any necessary punishing of children being too harsh. Locke warns us, commonsensically, that:

> . . . if the mind be curbed, and humbled too much in children; if their spirits be abased and broken much, by too strict an hand over them, they lose all their vigour and industry, and are in a worse state than the former. For extravagant young fellows, that have liveliness and spirit, come sometimes to be set right, and so make able and great men: but dejected minds, timorous and tame, and low spirits, are hardly ever to be raised, and very seldom attain to any thing.[16]

16. Locke, *Thoughts Concerning Education*, §46. Locke does sanction severe

Great men undertake human action in freedom. Dejected, timorous, and tame people of low spirits very seldom attain to any thing because they very seldom take ambitious, free, human action. They have been harmed; they have been broken. Their capacity for free action has been undermined. Their treatment has been abuse, a perversion of education.

Abuse is not discipline. It is not a part of education and it does not enhance freedom. Both psychological abuse and physical abuse are to be rejected. There is another form of abuse that must be rejected, too. It is a form that Enlightenment thinkers were much alive to—dogmatic abuse.

Immanuel Kant, for example, praised the prospect of a prince that would not abuse his people by imposing dogma.

> A prince who does not regard it as beneath him to say that he considers it his duty, in religious matters, not to prescribe anything to his people, but to allow them complete freedom, a prince who thus even declines to accept the presumptuous title of tolerant, is himself enlightened. He deserves to be praised by a grateful present and posterity as the man who first liberated mankind from immaturity (as far as government is concerned), and who left all men free to use their own reason in all matters of conscience.[17]

If such a prince is a liberator, the traditional prince who would impose dogma enslaves by dogmatic abuse, keeping his people immature, in a state of underdevelopment of their freedom and of their reason.

---

and harsh beating and domination only to counter obstinate disobedience and rebellion. Parenting and educating cannot go on in the face of this. If the rebellion goes on, parents, educators, and child live in a relationship different from parenting or educating. Such a relationship is not to be tolerated, "unless, for ever after, you intend to live in obedience to your son." §78.

17. Immanuel Kant, *An Answer to the Question, "What Is Enlightenment?"* trans. unknown (Konigsberg, Prussia: 30th September, 1784). (http://www.ets.uidaho.edu/mickelsen/texts/Kant%20-%20Enlightenment.txt.)

Six years later, the French mathematician and statesman, Condorcet, wrote eloquently about the potential for dogmatic abuse in a scheme of universal education that touched on political, moral, and religious opinions:

> Liberty of opinion in these matters would be merely an illusion if society laid hold of each generation to dictate what they must believe. The individual who enters society with opinions inculcated by his education is no longer a free man; he is a slave of his teachers. His chains are all the more difficult to break because he himself does not feel them; he thinks he is obeying his own reason when in fact he is only submitting to that of others.[18]

Education degraded to the mere transmission of a dogma to students is here seen as a form of enslavement. It works against the very skills and the freedom to use them at our own initiative that education is supposed to develop.

There are two lessons to be drawn from this fact. The first, quickly, is that while education has to transmit information to the student, it must primarily develop the skills of reasoning that let a person think for herself. Only through the exercise of reason is freedom—self-determination—possible.

Second, Condorcet inferred from the possibility of dogmatic abuse that education in political, moral, and religious matters must not be part of a universal scheme of education. He saw too great a potential for abuse if they were to be included in universal education of the youth of a society. He saw too much potential for an attack on human liberty if a central authority could insure that all people in a community would be trained in the same political, or ethical, or religious dogma. What all people are taught to believe, he thought, should be

---

18. Condorcet, *Public Instruction*, Part 3, §3.

"limited only to positive instruction, to the teaching of truths of fact and calculation."[19]

Condorcet anticipated a natural objection to what has just been advanced. The objection would be that if education in these matters is left to families there still will be indoctrination in dogma. It will just be family dogma! Some children will be indoctrinated by their families one way; others, from another family, in another; still others in other ways, and so on. The suggestion underlying this objection is that indoctrination in a family dogma is just as enslaving as would be a uniform indoctrination in a social dogma through a regime of universal education.

Condorcet reasonably thinks that this objection fails. He argues that even if we were to agree that all families will indoctrinate, the situation would be better than if a universal education agency were to have indoctrinated its dogma. His argument proceeds from the fact that if families indoctrinate different dogmas, the dogmatic, indoctrinated product of one family's indoctrination will grow up to profess a different dogma than that of another family's indoctrinated offspring. Then, in social interactions among the variously indoctrinated, differences of belief and lack of universality of dogma will become apparent to all, undermining in many the felt necessity of the dogmatic beliefs they were trained to hold.

The possibility of doubt's having entered one's mind Condorcet saw to be liberating in itself: "His [a dogmatist's] error, should he persist in it, is merely voluntary." It is up to him to determine the significance of the possibility of doubt. Condorcet thinks that societies in which many come to recognize the possibility of error among their dogmas are societies that come to have more free thinkers than dogmatists.

Condorcet made his case for freedom of thought and against uniform instruction in matters moral, religious, and political on epis-

19. Ibid.

temological grounds. His argument was that while family education schemes and universal education schemes are each liable to dogmatic abuse, indoctrinated people living in societies favoring family education in these matters are more likely to learn that they have been abused and so are more likely to reclaim their freedom and take steps to repair the harm done to them. People in a society where universal indoctrination had been practiced would be less likely to discover the inhibition of their freedom since everyone, everywhere will attest to the putatively obvious truth of everything that person believes.

Personal freedom, an aspect of human excellence, demands that there be no universal education in matters moral, religious, and political—or at least not much. I add that last modification because Condorcet overstepped his logic and his view should be modified.

There is an alternative to taking these matters completely out of universal education. One might, as we try to do now, work against the possibility of dogmatic abuse in a system of universal education by requiring that all in-system discussions of these matters have to be balanced, with a number of different viewpoints represented. It is hard to indoctrinate if one presents his own perspective as one of many possible views. Therefore, we could include discussions of morals, religion, and politics in a system of universal education, avoiding the potential abuse of indoctrination in dogma.

Now the question is: Given that we may include these topics in the domain of whatever universal education we provide children, should we do so? The answer to this question is yes—but not much.

We should leave thoroughgoing instruction in morals, religion, and politics outside the system of universal education. Education that develops virtue needs more rigorous advocacy of a vision of human excellence than any tepid presentation of many alternative views can afford. Education that develops virtue needs to be tailor-made for each child separately as, following Locke, I suggested above. I agree that education in ideals that will inform the character of a youth must be performed by caregivers who are not associated with the universal training of all the youth of a community, presumably by the parents in most cases.

Some small amount of discussion of alternative moral, religious, and political ideals, however, should remain part of the universal education for all children of a community. It should be included because we are inheritors of democratic institutions that the Enlightenment conferred on us. We who live in democratic societies are called upon to function together as citizen legislators. We live with an obligation to, and must train our children eventually to, take part in a public discussion of matters moral, religious, and political. We citizen legislators must set the direction of our institutions through deliberation with each other and through making many joint decisions in our societies.

Our children who we are educating to function excellently in these democracies must be initiated to the parameters of the discussion they are soon to enter. There must be some minimal common orientation of them to moral, religious, and political issues that they are likely to encounter in their future roles as citizen legislators. And there must be some broad outline presentation and discussion of methods for their jointly reasoning about these matters with their other future citizen legislators.

CHAPTER TWO

Public Education and Imperfect Democracy

Edwin G. West

OUR EDITOR Tibor Machan refers to the paradox wherein a country aspiring to be a fully free society tolerates the continuation of a coercive education system. The system is coercive because (a) it is funded, not by parental payments at the door of the school, but by mandatory taxes that are collected prior to the schooling, (b) students are legally forced to attend, (c) the choice of school is severely constrained. In the editor's words, "the paradox is that, despite all the negatives, folks have become very accustomed to public schools." I shall attempt to explain not only why public school systems invariably meet with the success so far indicated or, in other words, why radical reform seems currently to have only doubtful prospects. A brief initial focus will be on common historical origins of public government schooling worldwide, followed by a critical examination of the present situation from the standpoint of political economy and some assessment of prevailing economic analysis of the current roles of public and private education.

THE UNIVERSAL PATTERN OF EVOLUTION

In attempting to determine how, over 150 years, we still possess a monopoly public school system that provides a "one size fits all" education,[1] we shall start with a mental experiment. Consider an initial scenario in which education, like food, is being adequately demanded and supplied via an efficient private sector. How could ambitious politicians or administrators persuade government to intervene in the sense of obtaining for them a threshold of power? One can hypothesize at least two available methods. First, the potential interveners might produce plausible (even if erroneous) statistics showing areas of numerically deficient school attendance. The second method involves a call for respect for the "proper" boundaries of education and the exclusion of institutions that do not meet the officially approved definition of schooling. Such action will, of course, necessitate a full-time government department and an appropriate number of career civil servants and inspectors.[2]

STATISTICS OF EDUCATIONAL NEED:
THE CASE OF NEW YORK

The history of American education clearly demonstrates the two methods of intervention just described. In 1804 an act was passed providing that the net proceeds of the sale of five hundred thousand acres of the vacant lands owned by New York State be appropriated as a permanent fund (about $50,000 in value) for the support of

1. The phrase "one size fits all" is somewhat of an exaggeration because the "size" of public education in wealthy areas of the public system is usually "bigger" than elsewhere—but the phrase does give a correct impression in terms of mechanical uniformity of practice.

2. Jeremy Bentham and John Stuart Mill adopted both methods in advancing their strong criticisms of nineteeth-century British denominational instruction. (West, 1992, p. 598.)

schools. But how much support was actually needed? The answer lay in facts that had not yet been ascertained. To rectify this situation five commissioners were authorized in 1811 to report on a system for the establishment and organization of Common Schools. Their report appeared in 1812, accompanied by the draft of a bill that was the basis of the act passed later in that year. It is interesting to compare the terms of the bill with the rationale of state aid as argued in the report.[3] The commissioners acknowledged that, for state aid to be completely justified, it was necessary to establish in what respects the people were not already securing sufficient education for their children. They conceded immediately that schooling was indeed already widespread.

> In a free government, where political equality is established, and where the road to preferment is open to all, there is a natural stimulus to education; and accordingly *we find it generally resorted to, unless some great local impediments interfere.*[4]

Poverty was in some cases an impediment; but the biggest obstacle was bad geographic location:

> In populous cities, and the parts of the country thickly settled, *schools are generally established by individual exertion.* . . . It is in the remote and thinly populated parts of the State, where the inhabitants are scattered over a large extent, that education stands greatly in need of encouragement. The people here living far from each other, makes it difficult so to establish schools as to render them convenient or accessible to all. Every family therefore, must either educate its own children, or the children must forgo the advantages of education.[5]

---

3. J. Randall, *History of the Common School System of the State of New York.* Ivison, Blakeman, Taylor & Co., 1871, p. 18.
    4. Ibid., p. 18, my italics.
    5. Ibid., my italics.

The problem was thus presented in the same terms as those later to be used in England by W. E. Forster, the architect of the 1870 English Education Act; it was largely a problem, to use Forster's words, of "filling up the gaps." The logic of such argument, of course, called mainly for discriminating and marginal government intervention. To this end three policies were available: First, the government could assist families, but only the needy ones, by way of educational subsidies. Second, it could subsidize the promoters of schools in the special areas where they were needed. Third, the government itself could set up schools, but only in the rural "gap" areas. Without discussing possible alternatives, however, the commissioners promptly recommended that the inconveniences could generally best be remedied "by the establishment of Common Schools, under the direction and patronage of the State."

Thus, in place of discrimination in favor of poor and thinly populated districts, a flat equality of treatment was decreed for *all* areas; the public monies were to be distributed on a per capita basis according to the number of children between five and fifteen in each district, whether its population was dense or sparse. Beyond this, each town, at its own discretion, was to raise by tax, annually, as much money as it received from the school fund. It appears, therefore, that what the commissioners had succeeded in doing was guaranteeing, not the education of the most needy, but the emergence of an officially approved "nationalized" or "collectivized" education for rich and poor alike and in schools of homogeneous quality. Our editor's complaint of the "one size fits all" approach to education has thus (in the case of New York) been traced to its origins.

REQUIRED CONFORMITY WITH AMERICAN GOVERNMENT DEFINITIONS OF "EDUCATION"

As previously explained, the second method of intervention was to throw doubt on the quality of nonpublic education and to urge an *official* definition of "proper instruction." On the whole it was this strategem that dominated events in America because, in contrast to Britain, New York State in the early nineteenth century contained fairly clear statistical testimony to the fact that schooling was already widespread. The bureaucracies in this particular state, therefore, avoided the need for the misleading arithmetic being used in Britain that exaggerated the extent of educational negligence (West, 1992, pp. 603–9). Other kinds of forces, however, began inexorably to increase the relative strength of the public over the private school system. American public education was soon being called upon, not primarily, as in Britain, to produce a literate and fully employed population, but instead to condition young people to be independent of their families and to pursue the welfare not of individuals, but of the "nation." In so doing, the declared intention was to abolish all aspects of alleged inequity. Students from different backgrounds would be educated in "common" schools that produced "social cohesion." One of the associated functions of the schools, of course, was to "Americanize," if not homogenize, new immigrants from Europe.

Prominent in inculcating this new philosophy was Horace Mann who, in 1837, became the first secretary of the Massachusetts Board of Education. As Sheldon Richman observes: "For Mann, equalization and social harmony would be advanced by the compulsory mixing of children from rich and poor families" (Richman, 1995, p. 49). Clearly the existence of private schools that did not share such philosophy was an obstacle that, for Mann and his followers, had to be overcome.

A new government "weapon" was accordingly introduced into the struggle. Down to the 1860s parents using the public schools had been obliged to pay "rate bills" that amounted in financial terms to the equivalent of school fees. Under the "Free Schools Act" of 1867, however, the rate bills (fees) were abolished. This legislation had the desired result as far as the expanding public education bureaucracy was concerned. It consisted of the marginal "crowding out" of the private by the public sector. This occurred because when government schools are financed from tax funds and fees are abolished therein, the private sector cannot match the public action. In current terminology there was no longer "a level playing field."

Elementary economics predicts that artificial reduction of prices to zero leads to an erosion of appropriate incentives. Bearing in mind the growing monopoly status of the public schools, their administrators disliked one particular degree of freedom that had been left to dissatisfied parents. When the perceived quality of their schooling fell below a given level, they could often transfer their older children to nonformal schooling such as training on the job. Predictably the public education elites began to condemn such a "safety valve" and to demand laws for compulsory schooling. When governments take such action they are, of course, forced to *define* education. In practice this coincided with the type of education being supplied in conventional or standardized public schools. Other types were usually firmly ruled out.

This account of the emergence of compulsion again appears to explain in large part what has been the subsequent emergence of the "one size fits all" public education that so offends Tibor Machan and others today. The agitation by the teachers' association (and other interest groups) for compulsory laws, following the victory in 1867 of their Free School Campaign, was soon rewarded. The Compulsory Education Act was passed in 1874. Interestingly enough, after several years of operation it was declared ineffective. The Superintendent of 1890, asking for yet more legislation, complained that the existing laws were still not reaching the hard core of truant cases, those associated with dissolute families. Even this "hard core," however, was conceded to consist of a small minority: "It is worse than futile to assume that all persons charged with the care of children will send them to school. The great majority will."[6]

6. 36 Ann. Rep. N.Y. Supt. Public Instruction (1890), p. 35.

Whatever the fate of the children of the "hard-case" families, the final link in the process of monopolizing had now been firmly secured with respect to the education of all the other children, those in the vast majority of families, that were admitted to be fully responsible. Compulsory payment and compulsory consumption had become mutually strengthening monopoly bonds and the pattern of schooling for the next century had been firmly set.

POCKETS OF CURRENT RESISTENCE

Sheldon Richman (1995, p. 2) observes: "The public schools, despite their widely recognized problems, [today] have a mystique that prevents people from imagining a life without them." Questioning them, indeed, has come to be seen by some as audacious, if not irreverent; yet others believe that the system "has been an insidious assault on the integrity of the family" (Richman, 1995, p. 7). Has public education for the bulk of the population become a "necessary" institution simply because it is one of those institutions to which people have become accustomed? Whatever the case, the relevant bureaucracies have used their overwhelming influence to maintain the system and the status quo.

The power of today's government school bureaucracy can be measured partly by the level of current public education expenditure. With this at over $316 billion, education is now the second largest entitlement program in the United States (and the world), ranking behind Social Security but ahead of Medicare-Medicaid.[7] With money of this magnitude there is presumably more than enough for the public education system for self-advertisement and public relations programs together with formidable campaign power to resist all kinds of parental choice proposals. The power plus influence of the public system, meanwhile, extends to teacher training schools and education departments of universities, where most authors of histo-

7. Cardiff, 1996.

ries of education are to be found. If we are to achieve a full understanding of events, however, we must usually put aside the standard histories, which in the words of Mark Blaug "seem to have been largely written to prove that education is only adequately provided when the state [government] accepts its responsibility to furnish compulsory education *gratis*" (Blaug, 1975, p. 594).

OFFICIAL ATTEMPTS AT
RATIONALIZING THE SYSTEM

The favorite approach of public school advocates in attempting to rationalize the current public system is to assert that it is a crucial component of democracy. It is also urged that it is one that gives unique protection to the children of the poor. Such claims, however, are more expressions of faith than rationally argued and empirically demonstrated positions. To achieve the latter, the advocates need to address at least the following six questions:

1. If children's education needs the special protection of democracy, why do we not have similar protection in other areas such as government provision of free food, clothing, and shelter for children?

2. If parents are allowed to spend from their income directly on their child's food, why, in the case of schooling, is part of that income preempted by taxation to provide the *indirect* purchase of "free" schooling?

3. Again, if parents are allowed the opportunity to give their children immediate protection from an inferior food supply by promptly transferring their money and patronage from the inefficient store to a better one, why are they not allowed parallel powers to protect the education of their children?

4. How can one argue that democratic provision is necessary

for promoting equality of opportunity for the poor when, by preventing their families in ghetto schools from escaping to better schools, it perpetuates, if not aggravates, inequality of opportunity?

5. Why is it that the choice system that exists within the present system of heterogeneous public schools is available almost exclusively for the middle class and the rich? It is summarized by the words, "buy a house, buy a school."

6. Finally, since democracy is a simple *majority* voting institution, how can we expect the poor, who constitute a *minority*, to be particularly well served?

THE UNIONS

Another pertinent feature of democracy is the presence of alliances between governments (or political parties) and interest groups. In public education the foremost example is the teacher union. The sternest critics go so far as to complain that government schools are increasingly run by the unions and for the unions, but it is important first to analyze one of the most critical areas—that of collective bargaining. When looking for consistency in applying the principles of democracy (or rule by consent), one major factor that emerges is that, in practice, "collective bargaining in public education constitutes the negotiation of public policies with a special interest group [the union], in a process from which others are excluded. This is contrary to the way public policy should be made in a democratic representative system of government" (Lieberman, 1997, p. 64). As one conspicuous example, *The Chicago Tribune* has observed that the Chicago Teachers Association now has "as much control over operations of the public schools as the Chicago Board of Education . . . more control than is available to principals, parents, taxpayers, and voters." *The Tribune* claimed that curriculum matters, for instance, such as programs for teaching children to read, were written into the union contract. Indeed the board was required to bring *any* proposed changes to the bargaining table (Bovard, 1996, p. 498).

The leading unions, NEA and AFT, are strongly opposed to any policy that would introduce competition or would shrink the market for teacher services. "Thus the NEA/AFT oppose vouchers, tuition tax credits, contracting out, home schooling, or lowering the compulsory age limit for education . . . [and] are as adamnantly opposed to trial projects or demonstration projects as they are to large-scale programs to allow competition in the education industry" (Lieberman, 1997, p. 5). It should be noticed that such opposition to the programs described coincides with the strategies that any monopoly would adopt. Observers have to decide, therefore, whether the predominance of the unions' motive is the latter, or whether the union's education philosophy derives primarily from pursuit of the "public interest."

Simple majority democracies are associated with complex coalitions, large campaign-fund accumulations, and considerable vote-trading. The ability of well-organized and concentrated institutions to "deliver" vote support is, of course, a very attractive propensity to politicians. The NEA and the AFT are prominent examples. In 1972 the NEA organized its first political action committee (PAC), and by 1992 it was contributing over $2 million to congressional candidates. An additional $2 million, meanwhile, was going to state and national political parties for voter registration and related activities. In the opinion of Lieberman, while the unions do on occasion support Republicans, "for the most practical purposes, however, the NEA (and AFT) are adjuncts of the Democratic Party" (Lieberman, 1997, p. 76).

One final aspect of the workings of democracy needs explanation because it is invariably neglected. Specialists in the "economics of politics" observe that, in single-issue situations, the outcome of voting is determined by the median voter. Consider the following very sim-

TABLE I. Income Distribution: Five Individuals

Individual	Case A Income ($)	Case B Income ($)
1	1,000	1,000
2	2,000	2,000
3	3,000	3,000
4	4,000	4,000
5	5,000	10,000
TOTAL INCOME	15,000	20,000
Average income	3,000	4,000
Median income	3,000	3,000
Total proceeds of an education tax *of 10% of total income*	1,500	2,000

ple example of a population of five individuals with income distributions shown in table 1.

If each individual has a vote, then person number 3 is the median voter because there is an equal number of voters on either side of him. Assume that preferences for tax-funded education is distributed in proportion to income. Consider the median voter's preference to be m. Voters 4 and 5 will favor m over any proposal to supply less. Voters 2 and 1 will favor it over proposals to supply more. Thus the median voter's preference dominates.

In table 1 the median voter's income in case A is $3,000, and this is also the average income. Case B, in contrast, shows a "skewed" income distribution. The presence of exceptionally rich individual number 5 (with income of $10,000) increases the average income to $4,000. This is now $1,000 above the median income (which remains at $3,000). In the real world, income distributions are similarly skewed, although not as "severely."

Assume now that public education is financed by a flat tax equal to 10 per cent of income and that education costs $1 per unit. The median voter's education tax in scenario A would be $300, as would that of every other individual (since, to reiterate, the median voter's preference would dominate). The total education tax proceeds in case A therefore would be $300 \times 5 = \$1,500$. Each individual would obtain 300 units of education (bearing in mind that the assumed "tax price" or cost is $1 per unit).

Next suppose that the scenario changes from A to B. The total and average income would now increase to $20,000 and $4,000 respectively. The 10 per cent education tax would now generate a total of $2,000. This would allow the median voter to increase his demanded *quantity* of education to 400 units while still paying $300 in tax. In effect this is a drop in the median voter's tax price per unit of education. Because this "privilege" is available only through a tax-funded public education system, the median voter will, to that extent, be biased against any proposal to abolish it.

Alternatively, suppose that individual number 5 in table 1 (case B) was initially forfeiting a "free" public education for his child and instead was patronizing a fee-funded private school (that is, he was "paying twice" for his education). The total tax revenue available for public education would remain at $2,000. Spread now among only four users of public education, this would amount to an education worth $500 each. Consider next the probable response to a proposal to offer all parents, including those currently using private schooling, an education voucher worth $400 each. The median voter would clearly reject such a "universal voucher" because he would now be obliged to share the available total of education tax revenue with the rich individual (number 5). The conclusion is that, at least with such elementary models of politics, the forces of democracy would tend to resist such reforms as universal flat-rate vouchers.

Several critics of the public school system reject vouchers as a "solution" anyway because they foresee the future imposition of such a raft of regulatory standards that the recipient schools would become virtually indistinguishable from public schools. Even if one sides with these critics, however, it is necessary to appreciate that the above logic predicts an inherent resistance of the median voter public school supporter toward most other "solutions," including tax credits, contracting out, homeschooling, and lowering the compulsory age limit for education. Thus the typical concurrence in democracies of positively skewed income distributions, median voter dominance in single-issue situations, and the existence of some fee-funded private schooling, leads to the conclusion that the median voter is, to a large extent, gridlocked into the present public school system.

PESSIMISM VERSUS OPTIMISM

The overall thrust of this discussion tends toward what some would call pessimism. There are *some* developments, nevertheless, that deserve additional mention, especially since they might be viewed more optimistically. The first concerns the prediction (above) that the median voter will reject education vouchers when they are payable to all families. His opposition, however, may disappear if the vouchers are not universally available but are instead confined to low-income families. It so happens that it is this *selective* type of voucher that is featuring the successful system currently operating in Milwaukee.

Consider next the 1998 Supreme Court of Wisconsin's denial of the contention that the State's school-choice plans violate the Establishment Clause's separation of Church and State (*The Wall Street Journal*, Monday, Nov. 23, 1998). Clearly this decision will help to widen Milwaukee's voucher coverage. Indeed, family membership (enrollment) jumped from 1,500 in January 1998 to 5,695 in January 1999. Such success may well encourage other states, too. (The Wisconsin decision was appealed to the U.S. Supreme Court, which subsequently declared that it would not review the State Court's decision.)

CHARTER SCHOOLS

A third development that might be impressive to many is that of the charter schools. In the United States these are public schools that operate under state-enabling legislation and receive pupil funding from taxpayers' dollars, usually by allocation of district-level education funding on a per-pupil basis. Sponsors must apply to local education districts or a state authority for a charter under which they will function, stating educational objectives, curricula, and proposed methods of operating. Charter schools are governed locally by citizens, parents, teachers, and universities and are said to enjoy much autonomy. Some significant incentive effects exist because a charter is in effect a performance-based contract: If the school does not perform up to the standard set in the charter, its charter can be revoked and the school shut down. In the United States, 29 states now have charter laws, and by 1999 over 500 charter schools were in operation around the country. President Clinton has stated that the United States should set a goal of 3,000 charter schools by the year 2000.

Although many states have passed legislation that attempts to prohibit for-profit operators from chartering, this does not necessarily prevent for-profit companies from entering indirectly. Such companies may simply contract with the charter "holder" to operate a school. In the case of the successful for-profit private school organization called SABIS,[8] for example, although it has not been allowed to contract directly for a charter school in Chicago, it has got into the business indirectly by being hired as a charter school manager by a not-for-profit company. Elsewhere the for-profit mode appears to be spreading significantly. Of the 46 charter schools that began opera-

8. The name SABIS was constructed from the abbreviated surnames of the founders Leila Saad and Ralph Bistany. SABIS is an international chain of for-profit college prep schools with units in Lebanon, Pakistan, England, the United States, and five of the United Arab Emirates.

tion, for instance, in Arizona in 1995 to 1998, 13 are being run by for-profit organizations.

Clearly it is only a minority of charter schools that at present are run by for-profit organizations. Indeed, several states do not welcome even indirect association with them. It has to be remembered, meanwhile, that charter schools are public (government) schools, not private. With few exceptions—and the SABIS school seems to be one such—charter schools in most states are still hindered by a multitude of rules and procedures. Many lack access to capital and start-up funding. Some are forced to hand back significant portions of their budgets to the local district as a rent or overhead payment. It is not clear therefore that the typical charter school will be able to continue to operate with significantly less money than conventional public schools and simultaneously produce superior results. One should, in any case, keep the situation in the following numerical perspective: Even if the United States reaches President Clinton's stated goal of 3,000 such schools by the year 2000, there will still be some 80,000 public schools (over 96 per cent of the whole) that are not charter schools.

THE EDISON PROJECT

Another enterprise that has caused some excitement is the Edison Project, started by entrepreneur Christopher Whittle in 1992. Originally intended to produce a large national chain of private schools, it now focuses on negotiating contracts with public school districts to run individual schools for an established fee. The project now has contracts with 51 schools and serves more than 24,000 students in 26 communities. It hopes to have 75 contracted schools by the fall of 1999. This venture can be classified under the policy of "contracting out." Another example of it is the arrangement between Baltimore City and a company called Educational Alternatives, Inc. This endeavor, however, has not been very successful, the major problem being the toughness and political influence of the unions. They, of course, are generally opposed to any arrangement that does not guarantee strict observance of the unions' previously negotiated provisions such as salaries, curriculum, length of school day, and so on.

One striking aspect of the Edison Project is that it is beginning to offer stock options for teachers. The implication is that teachers will now have an opportunity to benefit financially from the success of their schools—an opportunity that has, of course, been blocked in the conventional public school system.

To return to the practice of contracting out, those education suppliers that attempt it seem always to be in a precarious and vulnerable position. If they try to demonstrate an ability to deliver education more efficiently—with lower costs—they soon find a serious obstacle in the fact that they have to respect the current practice of paying teachers, not in accordance with their success in the classroom, but instead according to length of experience and teacher education. The "new" education suppliers indeed tend to find themselves confronted with additional regulations at every turn. The main argument presented is that because "public money" is involved the newcomers must be shown to be "accountable." For more promising alternatives, it seems, choice advocates must look to experiments that are completely independent of public finance.

PRIVATELY FUNDED VOUCHERS

It so happens that in the United States there is a system of privately funded vouchers or scholarships independent of government funding. Predictably, it is on average operating with increased efficiency in education. This may well be due to the fact that the private funding of the vouchers is usually less than 100 per cent so that there is considerable room for contributions also from parents.

Major examples of particular programs occur in Milwaukee, San Antonio, Atlanta, and Battle Creek. In Milwaukee, the largest precollege scholarship program to date was launched with massive support from the Lynde and Harry Bradley Foundation and the Archdiocese of Milwaukee. In its first year, the Milwaukee program served more than 2,000 students. In the same year in San Antonio a group of business leaders, in conjunction with the Texas Public Policy Foundation, launched a private voucher program serving over 900 students.

Although it has some very attractive features form the point of view of those who favor market competition, the privately funded voucher system could not possibly hope to make substantial inroads on the public education system in the near future. The main reason is the limitation of voluntary donation funds. The story may differ, however, in the *long run* after generations of families have been presented with successive demonstration effects about how to deliver quality education.

HOMESCHOOLING

A final example of interesting developments is that of homeschooling. Estimates suggest that up to 1.23 million families are now educating their children at home, and that the growth rate is between 15 and 40 per cent per year.[9] Motives vary from concerns about crime and lack of discipline in government schools to general dissatisfaction with their preformance. According to Lyman (1998), the lesson from the current boom is that "homeschooling, with minimal government interference, has produced literate students at a fraction of the cost of any government program."

Bearing in mind that, logically, education is an issue of states' rights, laws and regulations vary. In states such as Idaho, Oklahoma, and Texas there is no requirement for parents to initiate contact to

9. Lyman, 1998.

begin homeschooling. On the other hand, states such as Massachusetts, Minnesota, and New York are heavily regulated.

THE ECONOMISTS

The twentieth-century economic case for vouchers was first presented by Milton Friedman (1962). He focused on inefficiencies in the public school system stemming from its monopoly status. Thirty-seven years later such complaints persist and frustration among Friedman's followers seems undiminished. Economist Eugenia Toma (1999) emphasizes the continued lack of appropriate incentives. Where productive changes do occur, those responsible are often left without rewards. This is because the process of generating change is so diffuse that the individual innovators cannot be identified. In addition, those among the suppliers who fail to provide education have been exempt from responsibility, protected as they are by their unions. "Substantive educational policy changes most often have stemmed from the state level of government and from bureaucrats far removed from the production process. . . . When policies do change, they tend not to be marginal. We switch from phonics to whole word reading or from old math to new math, and to the classroom teacher, these changes appear overnight and without his or her input" (Toma, p. 5).

Toma's proposed reform is the most radical so far: Together with vouchers she would introduce the following major structural change: "Assign private ownership rights over the schools by giving them to the teachers and their unions. Make the teacher unions residual claimants in the strongest sense of the term. By owning the schools, the teachers and union members will face incentives that coincide with the incentives of parents and taxpayers" (p. 15). A key question to pose here, however, is whether the present agents in the system will accept the offered donation, bearing in mind the implied loss of their present protected position.

Other economists find Friedman's diagnosis inadequate because they believe that it does not sufficiently take into account the public ("external") as distinct from private benefits. The externalities from education are said to include the benefits enjoyed by a persons/ taxpayers outside the immediate family. The education of a family's child improves the welfare of such "neighbors" because, for instance, (a) the implied acquisition of literacy makes for a more democratic and stable society; (b) there is less crime; (c) the production of human capital redounds to the economic success of the whole society. Because such externalities can stem equally from private schooling, however, there are no clear-cut policy implications. Friedman has in fact always recognized the theories of externalities but has stressed the need for precise evidence. Some citizens, especially in the violent of school year of 1999, might focus on the possibility that externalities from public, as distinct from private, schooling can sometimes be substantially negative.[10]

Manski (1992) contends that "to Milton Friedman, the theoretical argument for vouchers was sufficiently compelling to make empirical evidence unnecessary..." (p. 354). On the contrary, Friedman insists that evidence is crucial, especially with respect to claims about externalities. A key consideration is whether externalities are "policy relevant" at the margin, and this can be demonstrated *only* by evidence. Since this is not produced by Friedman's critics, it appears

---

10. George Will has emphasized (*This Week with Sam Donaldson and Cokie Roberts*, Sunday, April 28, 1999) that the growing instances of violence, such as the massacre at Colombine High School on April 20, occur in the *public schools*. It would be difficult, he maintained, to conceive of student gangs wearing trench coats ever to be allowed in private schools (where firmly imposed dress codes typically prevail). He also expressed the view that any attempt to prevent public school students from bringing swastikas to school would immediately invite the opposition of the Civil Liberties Union. One should remember, too, that the typical size of government schools is well above that in the private system, a fact that tends to depersonalize education. It seems therefore that insofar as there are externalities associated with public schooling, several of them might well be adverse.

that it might be they who are empirically wanting. In the meantime, Friedman (1975, p. 92) observes "I have yet to see a plausible argument for any net positive marginal externality from additional schooling."[11]

THE STUDENT PEER GROUP PROBLEM

Several economists are now researching one particular case of negative externalities that involves what are called peer group effects. When a bright student from a public school moves to a private school (with the aid of a voucher) he or she will stimulate other students in the new school such that overall achievement will improve. Less bright students, however, who are left in their original public school will suffer a reduction in stimulus because of the emigration of their motivated and more able colleagues. These economists stress that such negative external effects violate the policy objective of providing *equality* of educational benefits (from vouchers) across students. In short, while vouchers increase efficiency they offend equity. Thus Dennis Epple and Richard Romano (1998), while affirming "the obvious claim" that vouchers will stimulate competition and thereby "reduce technical inefficiencies," contend that the resultant peer group effect will nevertheless induce a school hierarchy to the detriment of the least-able students. (See also Nechyba [1998] and Manski [1992].)

This last statement has to be qualified by the observation that the

11. For those having difficulty with the concept of marginal externality consider the following: Suppose medical research has established the probability that if the average person eats one orange a month he will benefit not only himself but also other persons in his environment. The implications for government policy will then depend on the evidence of private consumption. If people are on average already eating *two* oranges a month, then nothing further is to be gained from government intervention. The external benefits are irrelevant at the margin. This is Friedman's position with regard to education, and it has been influenced by his reading of the historical evidence of private behavior with respect to schooling before intervention.

public system itself has also induced school hierarchies. The system is *not* homogeneous, and this fact is eventually acknowledged in Epple and Romano (1998). As Toma (1999) observes, upper-income children "live in nice suburban homes and consume the best the public system has to offer. They get the best buildings, the best teachers, the most rigorous curriculum, and the widest variety of extracurricular activities" (p. 7). The affluent parents of such children, meanwhile, benefit from the deductibility of their school taxes.

THE RELEVANCE OF SMALL- VERSUS LARGE-SCALE VOUCHERS

The economist Manski (1992) prescribes two complementary ways to learn the effects of *choice*. One is to undertake experiments with voucher systems but, he insists, they must be carried out on something like the scale of contemplated operational systems. The second approach is to undertake simulations based on "plausible models of the behavior of the relevant actors. . . ." (p. 357). The tendency of such economists seems to be to focus on large-scale voucher systems together with the apparently "all-inclusive" simulation method on the grounds that actual experiments, such as the Milwaukee voucher, are too narrow in scope. This dismissal of the latter plan is unfortunate, however, because all of the "simulation economists" mentioned focus primarily on the needs of the poor, and it so happens that the seven-year-old means-tested Milwaukee voucher plan has concentrated exclusively on the welfare of this same minority.

Evidence from the Annual Reports by John F. Witte shows in fact that most families using the vouchers to obtain access to private schools are among the poorest. Their average income happens, indeed, to be about only half the level of the average Milwaukee public school family. With regard to the propensity of vouchers to "skim the cream," Witte concludes that the progam has been offering opportunities primarily to poor families "whose children were not succeeding in public school." One factor meanwhile that tends to be over-looked by economists relates to overall cost. In the first four years of the Milwaukee program, the value of the voucher was around $3,000, while the public school costs per student were approximately $6,000. This yielded a benefit/cost ratio of two to one if we assume that student achievements between private and public education remained constant—which was Witte's conclusion.[12]

Having stated that on the one hand vouchers may cause peer quality in public schools to decline while, on the other, public school quality may improve due to "competitive pressures on an inefficient public system," Nechyba (1998) concludes that a "classic tradeoff" is involved. (See also Manski, 1992, p. 357.) The existence of a tradeoff, however, does not guarantee that a trade will actually take place. It all depends on the asking (or reservation) prices involved. To take an extreme example: If the "price" of maintaining the peer quality for a minority in public schools is, say, 90 per cent of GDP, a "trade" would surely be out of the question. This example brings up the question of the approximate price, or cost, of forgoing a voucher system in order to protect the current balance of peer quality in public schools. The Milwaukee experience suggests that the authorities would be abandoning the opportunity of a very low for a very high cost of education supply. Whether the voucher policy should or should not be adopted is obviously very debatable from the tradeoff point of view. Yet such important cost issues appear to be surprisingly ignored (or played down) by the "simulation analysts" so far mentioned.

It is difficult not to conclude that the "new" (post-Friedman) economists might be straying from the most meaningful and constructive avenues of analyses. Consider next their insistence that

12. Econometric research by Rouse (1996) concludes that up to that year the Milwaukee Parental Choice program had increased math scores in voucher schools by between 1.5 and 2 percentage points per year, while the results for reading scores were mixed.

voucher experiments be carried out on something like the scale of contemplated (large) operational systems (Manski, 1992; Nechyba, 1999). This appears to brush on one side too quickly the striking success of small local experiments such as that in Milwaukee. In addition some of their arguments are vague. They appear, for instance, to visualize exclusively a top-down imposition of equality by something they describe as "society." This institution is never defined, even though one could explore several versions—including society consisting of the (unionized) suppliers of education, society as determined by median voters, or society as viewed in terms of unanimous consent in a constitutional setting.[13]

Can we really dismiss the Milwaukee project because it doesn't involve "the scale of the contemplated system"? Why couldn't the local (Milwaukee) area be the relevant scale contemplated? Now firmly established, it can yield valuable insights for other localities that wish to start their own experiments. Economists have lost perspective if they have in mind the federal authorities as being the only possible architects of a voucher system. Among other things, this would ignore the legal fact that the U.S. Constitution has given the main responsibility for education to state and *local* governments.[14]

It is intriguing to conjecture what would have happened had the new economists' approach been attempted on the eve of the replacement of the nineteenth-century network of universal private (and denominational) schools by a system of common schools financed partly by taxes and partly by fees. Would there have been any inhibition then because of the absence of any extensive experiment "on the scale of the truly contemplated ('free public') system"? From our knowledge of the history of educational events the answer seems to

13. Manski (1992, p. 355) refers to "society" seven times on the same page without providing a single definition.

14. Manski (1992) justifies dismissal of the Milwaukee evidence partly on the grounds that "these efforts have not been in place long enough for conclusions to be drawn" (p. 354). But this comment was made seven years ago.

be no. The system that emerged was due largely to the efforts of the "society" of the organized teaching profession. This scenario is a far cry from visions of a top-down establishment of a truly equitable education system by some benevolent government.

In the meantime, even if the economists' propositions about the negative externalities of peer group effects are acceptable in terms of pure logic, their implication for the real world must at present be seen as rather remote. The chief objective of Epple and Romano (1998), for instance, was to devise the best *design* for a voucher, one that resolves the peer group problem. Epple and Romano's basic idea is that vouchers vary in value with ability—that is, their value rises as student ability declines. No voucher is given to those who are the least needy—to those, in other words, who attend higher-quality schools. Obviously the information and administration requirements will be large. And the fact remains that it is a voucher system that is ultimately being recommended by Epple and Romano, and one that does not seem to promise to reduce at all the opposition to vouchers by teacher unions and administrators.

It appears, in fact, that the strength of very local politics accounts for more success in the establishment of vouchers than the presentation of abstract economic theories. It should be remembered that the Milwaukee plan was pioneered largely by the Democratic representative "Polly" Williams to remove the inequity on her poor constituents by giving them the advantage of public/private choice that only the middle class was enjoying. This has been one of the rare cases in democracy when the poor have received direct political support in their council chambers. Just as interesting, the Milwaukee plan, once established, triggered wide institutional support. It did, after all, prompt the Supreme Court to clarify much further the probable constitutional status of school choice plans under the Establishment Clause. If it had not been for the existence of the Milwaukee plan this might not have happened.

Any attempt to give priority to the "new economists'" policy of optimal redistribution of student peers must first demonstrate that the administrative costs will not be prohibitive. Notice, too, that the policies suggested so far concentrate on those educational "outputs" that are easy to measure. In a world of rigidly confined public education, this will be relatively easy to accomplish. Where, however, the objective is to relax the associated coercion by reinstating parental freedom to choose, one can expect the introduction of a rich diversity of educational processes, many of which are *not* easy to measure in terms of "outputs" and consumer satisfaction. Thus the complaint that the "peer group effect" will induce a school hierarchy to the detriment to the least able students is open to the challenge that the latter group, as well as all other families, might be more than compensated by their new access to private types of education that cater to a wider spectrum of cultural aspirations, philosophies, and religions, together with a closer and more workable matching of individual students with teachers. Where education vouchers are a fact of life, new private schools can be expected to spring up quite rapidly and in a wide variety of places to meet newly expressed demands. Further, the competition that Epple and Romano expect from vouchers, together with what they call a reduction of the technical inefficiencies that it will bring, might more than compensate taxpayer/citizens for any negative peer group effect. Notice too that such an effect will not occur where the value of an existing public education is zero. If advocacy groups are correct, for instance, thousands of students, mainly Blacks and Hispanics who live in the poorest neighborhoods, experience such deplorable conditions in New York that entire school districts are being labeled "dead zones."[15]

The fact that the Milwaukee experience reveals that vouchers unleash a variety of enthusiastic new demands is borne out by the evidence. Witte's reports include the finding, for instance, of high

---

15. "New York's Schools Ignite Political Showdown," *The Globe and Mail* (Toronto), p. A14, June 7, 1999.

parental involvement and satisfaction, once in the voucher system. Agreement among parents that the program should continue has been almost unanimous (McGroaty, 1994, p. 110). It is not surprising that, since its inception, lack of space has resulted in more students being turned away than have been accepted into the plan so that, in consequence, spaces are now apportioned by lottery.

CONCLUSION

The first part of this discussion explored, in historical terms, the evolution of the public education system as we know it today. Desiring to place the system in the arena of politics, ambitious opportunists in the nineteeth century used two approaches. The first was the brandishing of statistics claiming serious educational deficiency, a method that was used especially in Britain. The second method, used more especially in the United States under such leaders as Horace Mann, was to condemn the nature and content of the hitherto flourishing private schooling. It was now insisted that private schools were not in a position to offer the "true" kind of education.

No apology is made for the sustained historical account at the beginning of this discussion because we can now see history repeating itself in the reappearance of such arguments. According to one specialist in the child care area, advocates of increased government involvement in this field "generally argue that (1) there is a shortage of child care facilities, (2) unregulated child care is harmful to children."[16] As we have seen, these are precisely the two types of arguments that proved so successful in obtaining government intervention in the nineteenth century. According to my analysis of the latter situation, the empirical evidence did not support the offered rationale. Apparently (see Olsen, 1997), the same is true today.

Staunch supporters of the public school system today attempt to

16. Olsen (1997), p. 1.

rationalize it via a series of further *a priori* arguments. A leading one is the assertion that public schools have become necessary institutions because they are an essential part of democracy. Our work, however, has posed six questions that tend to challenge this assumption on its own grounds. Beyond this, a full description of democracy calls for a proper investigation of government alliances in the real world with interest groups such as teacher unions. As conducted today, it has been maintained that these institutions are often serious *obstacles* to democracy. A second avenue of rationalization of the government system, and one that is being pursued by some economists, is the claim that the same enterprise can best handle the student peer group problem.

Reference has been made to two schools of economists on the subject of educational policy. The older one has been that of Milton Friedman and the younger has featured neoclassical model builders. Uncomfortable at what they see as a current lack of supply of real evidence on vouchers, and demanding a strict emphasis on analysis rather than advocacy, the latter group has resorted to mathematical simulation in terms of large-scale models. We have conjectured here that the Friedman school would not agree that there is a serious absence of useful evidence, and it would cite the Milwaukee Plan as a case in point.

It is now time, however, to draw attention to another important distinction. Friedman regards the education voucher simply as a stepping-stone to the ultimate withdrawal of government in education (except for providing for the really destitute).[17] Friedman's voucher will initially be valued at something less than the average per capita cost of public education. With the passage of time the proportion of the voucher value to the average public cost will diminish, eventually reaching zero. Private enterprise will then begin to flourish again because of the restoration of a level playing field.

17. Milton and Rose Friedman (1980), p. 162.

The second school of economists is obviously reluctant to enter this dimension of the debate. To the Friedmans, on the contrary, it is the long-term objective or vision that is the most crucial. It brings more into the open the teacher unions' assumption that a market-driven public education system catering mainly to parents and families would be seriously misinformed because it would weaken the influence of trained and unionized personnel. The latter, after all, claim to be "professional educators" while parents cannot make such a claim, and certainly parents do not have the time to deliberate on the best pedagogic requirements for their children.

The Friedman school strongly challenges this viewpoint, and the second school appears to ignore it. The most outspoken defender of parents and families in the history of political economy was Sir Robert Lowe, a writer with whom the Friedman group will evidently feel much affinity. Lowe told the 1868 School Enquiry Commission in Britain, "I myself see nothing for it but to make the parents of the children the ministers of education, and to do everything you can to give them the best information as to what is good education, and where their children can be well taught, and to leave it to work itself out." The precise reasons for this judgment were expressed by Lowe later in the same year:

> Parents have one great superiority over the Government or the administrators. . . . Their faults are mainly the corrigible faults of ignorance, not of apathy and prejudice. They have and feel the greatest interest in doing that which is for the real benefit of their children. They are the representatives of the present, the living and acting energy of a nation, which has ever owed its sure and onward progress rather to individual efforts than to public control and direction. They have the wish to arrive at a true conclusion, the data are before them, they must be the judges in the last resort, why should we shrink from making them judges at once?[18]

18. Robert Lowe (1868), p. 24.

REFERENCES

Annual Nineteenth Century Reports of New York Superintendents of Public Instruction.

Becker, Gary S. (1995). "Human Capital and Poverty Alleviation," HRO Working Paper, World Bank (March).

Blaug, Mark (1975). "The Economics of Education in English Classical Political Economy: A Re-Examination," in A. Skinner and T. Wilson, *Essays on Adam Smith*, Oxford: Clarendon Press, p. 595.

Bovard, James (1996). "Teachers' Unions: Are the Schools Run for Them?" *The Freeman* (July).

Cardiff, Chris (1996). "Education: What about the Poor?" *The Freeman* (July).

Epple, Dennis, and Richard Romano (1998). "Educational Vouchers and Cream Skimming," Carnegie Mellon University Working Paper.

Friedman, Milton (1962). *Capitalism and Freedom*, Chicago: University of Chicago Press.

Friedman, Milton and Rose (1980). *Free to Choose*. New York: Harcourt, Brace and Jovanovich.

Lieberman, Myron (1997). *The Teacher Unions*. New York: The Free Press.

Lowe, Robert (1868). *Middle Class Education: Endowment or Free Trade?* London: Bush.

Lyman, Isabel (1998). *Homeschooling: Back to the Future?* Policy Analysis, No. 294. Washington, D.C.: CATO Institute.

Manski, Charles F. (1992). "Educational Choice (Vouchers) and Social Mobility," *Economics of Education Review*, Dec. 11 (4), pp. 351–69.

McGroaty, D. (1994). "School Choice Slandered," *Public Interest* 117 (Fall), pp. 94–111.

Nechyba, Thomas J. (1998). "Mobility and Private School Vouchers." Department of Economics Working Paper, Stanford University.

Olsen, Darcy (1997). "The Advancing Nanny State." *Policy Analysis*, No. 285. Washington, D.C.: CATO Institute.

Randall, J. (1871). *History of the Common School System of the State of New York*. New York: Ivison, Blakeman, Taylor & Co., p. 18.

Richman, Sheldon (1995). *Separating School and State*. Fairfax, Va.: The Future of Freedom Foundation.

Rouse, C. E. (1996). "Private School Vouchers and Student Achievement: An Evaluation of the Milwaukee Parental Choice Program." Working Paper No. 371. Princeton: Princeton University, Industrial Relations Section.

Toma, Eugenia F. (1999). "Will Johnny Read Next Year?" Fifteenth Annual Lecture in the Virginia Political Economy Lecture Series, March 18.

West, Edwin G. (1975). *Nonpublic School Aid*. Lexington, Mass.: Lexington Books.

West, Edwin G. (1992). "The Benthamites as Educational Engineers," *History of Political Economy*, 24:3.

West, Edwin G. (1994). *Education and the State*, London: Institute of Economic Affairs, 1965; 2d ed., 1970, 3d ed. (revised and extended), Indianapolis: Liberty Fund, 1994.

CHAPTER THREE

Schools and Education:
Which Children Are Entitled to Learn?

Carol B. Low

PUBLIC SCHOOLS are a fact of life in today's United States—like death and taxes, inevitable. Yet if one sits in with a group of parents discussing their children's schooling, one is likely to hear myriad complaints. The complaints are not the same from the parents around the table. One says her child is having a problem and the school refuses to provide the special services to which he is entitled. The next says his child is gifted and the school has a gifted enrichment program, but his child is still restless. Another says his child is falling behind and the teacher is going too fast, while another says her child is bored. Still others make it known that their children are in the wrong class, that the teacher is too strict, too lenient, too loud, too quiet. Many complain that their children have too much homework and that *they* do not have time to sit with their children and get all of it done. There are minor complaints, as well—the school is too big or too small, the school has not given the children time off for this holiday or that, vacation is too long or too short. And, of course, for some, the curriculum ignores their important religious upbringing while for others the curriculum is too biased in favor of one certain morality and religion, and even a certain calendar and holidays! Yet others complain that the school is teaching morality—drug and sex issues that they prefer to teach at home. There are nearly as many different complaints as there are individuals in the room.

The children complain also. They complain about too many hours in school. They complain about too much homework. They complain about rules that become more stringent and less logical every year. They complain about the loss to their freedom. And they even complain about the myriad tests many states and localities have instituted with the ostensible purpose of holding the schools accountable for providing adequate education. Interestingly enough, teachers are also heard to complain about this last item. Although this might amaze their pupils, some teachers want to teach more and obey rules less, as well! So it appears that among the groups most affected by public schools, there is much complaint and much dissension.

Indeed, these complaints are no surprise when we take every child in the United States at some age between 5 and 8 and begin a process of trying to educate them all in the same way, on the same schedule, by the same people with the same training! What is surprising is that Americans have become so conditioned to the concept of public schooling and, indeed, formal schooling in general, that they begin with the assumption that Johnny or Susie must necessarily be in this institution or their parents will have to take on a hefty private school tuition! How many say, "Well, since Johnny is not getting the education I wish him to have, I shall take him out of school entirely"? Not many, to be sure, though the number is on the rise. In 1990, about 300,000 children were reportedly homeschooled. By 1996, the number was estimated to have risen to nearly one million.[1] It is important to ask why so many continue to fight the futile fight for their child to get *exactly* the education they need and deserve out of a "one size fits all" system. It is important to ask why so many sit helplessly by while their children struggle in the current system. It

1. Brian D. Ray, "Fact Sheet 2b" (Salem, Ore.: National Home Education Research Institute, June 1997).

is important to ask why, while more and more families are opting out to private schools and homeschooling every year, on the whole, relatively few select these options. What is the belief system that is allowing children to be sacrificed to this struggling system generation after generation?

The easy answer to the above questions is that parents and other taxpayers believe, quite sincerely, that schools are full of professionals who know how to educate children and that parents do not know how to educate children, and that therefore children must stay in school for their own good. Parents are afraid to raise their own children—a thing that other parents did for generations before public school was mandated. Now sincerity in such an important area of life is a good thing, and it is certainly not the case that most parents are lazy or uncaring. In fact, although many use the argument that we must have public schools because of the many people who *are*, indeed, lazy and uncaring and would not educate their children, this does not bear up under scrutiny. In the past in this country, many people were educated or educated themselves quite competently at home and in private libraries or private schools. The reality of today is that these parents have lived all of their lives in a society in which public school is the norm, and they simply cannot conceive of what it would be like to take full responsibility for such a monumental task as the education of a child. After all, if the entire government cannot get it right, what is one parent or one family to do?

Thus, most parents do not balk when they get the summons from the local school enrolling their son or daughter in kindergarten—interestingly, even when they have a choice. In most states, kindergarten is not mandatory, and in some, the first grade or two are not, either! Many parents are already concerned that their five- or six-year-old children may fall behind in their learning or not get the proper social environment or feel left out when the other children in the neighborhood tramp off to school. It is also true that both parents are often working out of the home to earn enough to pay the taxes for this school and the rest of the government programs they support, so they are glad their children will be in the right place while they scurry off to work. Today's families often feel they have little choice when it comes to using public schooling for their children.

The following pages will explore the fallacy of public schooling. Just what is wrong with the assumptions that children must be in school from an early age, that the schooling must be provided by government, and that the government is best able to do so? Mass education rests upon many assumptions—that girls and boys are the same, that all children can be taught in the same way, that more schooling is better than less, that more money will fix problems that less fails to solve, and that teachers, as they are now defined, are best qualified to teach the children of the United States. What is the truth about each of these assumptions, and what are the results of resting the leviathan of public schooling upon them? What happens to children who are treated to a "one size fits all" system, who are labeled and sorted according to some artificial criteria, and who are faced with fixed demands regarding what they can learn and how they should do so? With the minds of children at stake, it is vital to look at public schooling, question the assumptions upon which it rests, and seek options that might enhance the process of education but do no harm.

CHILDREN ARE PEOPLE, TOO

Girls and Boys

Problems with generalized education begin to manifest immediately. To most observers, there are obvious differences between girls and boys, in both anatomy and behavior. Our current system, however, which undertakes their education at an early age, treats both sexes exactly the same. This is the fallacy of assuming that the obvious differences are the only differences. A cursory look at psychological and educational literature indicates that girls and boys are exactly the same in the dimensions relevant to education, that there is no difference in intelligence, behavior, or learning style; no difference in potential and no difference in strengths and weakness by sex. There are research and test results and statistics which support this. However, a closer look shows something else entirely. There are differences. Just as boys and girls do not look the same, due to genetic differences that began to create them as boy or girl from early in prenatal development, those differences are reflected in subtle ways throughout their brains and bodies. Statistics by definition are generalizations. We can use them to demonstrate pretty much anything, but in the case of male/female differences, careful use of the statistical analyses reveals that there are, indeed, differences between populations of girls and populations of boys. Saying that there are differences in style or capability between samples of girls and boys does not mean, for example, that there are no girls who fit what we might call the "boy" profile, or boys that fit the "girl" profile in terms of learning style and likes, dislikes, and behavior. Looking at generalizations, the point can be made that girls and boys in myriad subtle and not-so-subtle ways, are different. This fact has ramifications for how we should educate them.

The corpus of psychological and sociological literature goes through some dramatic contortions and rationalizations to make test results come out the same for girls and boys. It would be wrong— politically incorrect—to arrive at conclusions that depict differences. Such discoveries could be used as justification to discriminate in college applications or job placement or even course placement by sex, so the scores must look the same. Thus, the SATs are changed year after year to show no differences between boys and girls or children of different backgrounds.[2] As a result, they are now known

---

2. Alan S. Kaufman, *Assessing Adolescent and Adult Intelligence*, Boston: Allyn & Bacon, 1990), p. 54.

to reflect achievement more than potential or ability, which has even caused American Mensa to stop using them as a criterion for admission. Over the years, standardized tests such as achievement and personality and aptitude tests have been altered and renormed to attempt to eliminate discrimination between races and sexes.[3] Here, however, we come upon a problem with the definition of "discrimination." When used properly, the word denotes the making of fine distinctions. Modern usage adds "unfair" to that definition, but the point must be made that if tests do not discriminate between test-takers, then what are they for? The questions and the means of standardization of certain types of tests have been changed over and over to prevent differences from cropping up between races, between sexes, with the effect that genuine differences are eliminated from view. The fact, of course, is that tests cannot eliminate differences; they can simply bury them in the statistics. However, if we go below the surface, the mere fact that it takes such effort to make these test scores equilibrate between the sexes is telling us that there are differences that are not being depicted adequately. There are simply things at which girls are better than boys and things at which boys are better than girls, and there are things that they simply approach differently. Interestingly, these things may change with development and education, but at any given stage of development, there are sex differences on a statistically significant level between populations of boys and girls—things that should affect how we teach them!

As a Montessori teacher, the author was often struck by the consistent differences observed when teaching boys and girls to read and do mathematics. It was surprisingly clear that most boys loved working with and understanding numbers and somehow disliked letters and working with letters, at least visually. Girls generally could be predicted to spend more time with letters, learning their sounds, placing letter cutouts down to spell words and, soon, even reading at

3. Ibid., p.156.

very young ages. Boys learned the sounds as easily, but appeared to be bored by the letters when placing and reading entered the project. The author's own children also showed this difference dramatically. Their mom, the Montessori teacher, followed the well-established protocols, and all of these delightfully gifted children could read at age two or two-and-a-half. However, while the two girls instantly began reading *Hop on Pop* and progressively more difficult materials, up to and including *Heidi*, at age nine, the boy was finished, disinterested, in short order. He had met the challenge of learning the letter sounds and *could* read; he just didn't—for five years. Somewhere around his seventh birthday, he picked up a Hardy Boys book and polished it off, launching voluntarily into a love of reading unequaled by his sisters. Before he rediscovered reading, however, he thoroughly humiliated his two-and-a-half-year-older sister by learning long division first, without ever having been taught it!

Had these unscientific results from both home and school not presented the same basic pattern, they should have been chalked up to individual differences and, perhaps, some observer bias. Further study was definitely called for. There were more observed differences—was it this writer's culturally biased imagination, or were boys more active, more interested in cars and trucks and things mechanical and girls more interested in sedentary activities and pleasing adults? The generalizations seemed to fit the author's classroom experience over the years, feminist writers notwithstanding. Again, at home, with the ability to control the environment and the exposure more closely, there became little doubt that something not strictly cultural was different. Armed with a great sandbox, a load of the most wonderful Tonka trucks on the market at the time, and lots of patience, the author set out to give the firstborn—a girl—every opportunity to find her love of things mechanical. She didn't—preferring pots and pans and dolls from the beginning. When her little brother came along, before he could walk or talk, he promptly appropriated all of the trucks, scooting them along from a kneeling position, and spoke his first word: "Vroom."

Although this entertaining anecdotal data is psychologically convincing, it is not statistically significant. There are, however, research data to add support. In the literature, there is a tendency to play down the importance of findings that point out male/female differences, but they do appear, nonetheless, in the data. As seen in the hands-on teaching experience, boys and girls enter what Montessori called "sensitive periods" for reading and mathematics at different times and even with a different developmental substrate—so while girls appear to take on reading as a visual project, boys appear to take it to be an auditory project. Girls also tend to do math as a linear visual project, while boys are more mechanical or spatial in their approach. This is reflected in differences in subtest scores on such tests as the WISC-R, a standard and highly regarded IQ test for children.[4] Looking briefly, then, at research about general trends of male/female differences, some physiological measures have indicated that females may have a bigger corpus callosum, especially at the region called the splenium, which correlates with enhanced verbal reasoning.[5] Males, in general, are better at mechanical/spatial rotation,[6] and have a more fully developed hemispheric separation.[7] Again, this does not prevent some girls from surpassing some or all boys in visuo-spatial skills or some boys from surpassing most or all

4. Alan S. Kaufman, *Intelligent Testing with the WISC-R* (New York: John Wiley & Sons, 1979), p. 118.

5. Melissa Hines, Lee Chiu, Lou A. McAdams, Peter M. Bentler, et al., "Cognition and the corpus callosum: Verbal fluency, visuospatial ability, and language lateralization related to midsagittal surface areas of callosal subregions," *Behavioral Neuroscience* 106 (1992): 3–14.

6. Nordvik Hilmar and Benjamin Amponsah, "Gender differences in spatial abilities and spatial activity among university students in an egalitarian educational system," *Sex Roles* 38 (1998): 1009–23.

7. Martin Reite, Jeanelle Sheeder, Peter Teale, M. Richardson, Matthew Adams, and Jack Simon, "MEG based brain laterality: Sex differences in normal adults," *Neuropsychologia* 33 (1995): 1607–16.

girls at early verbal skills. These data are generalizations intended to offer a picture of how we can better serve young people based upon their differences as well as their likenesses.

It also appears to be the case that the different hormonal environments in brain and body lead to different behavioral styles and preferences, naturally. Studies with young mammals indicate consistently that there are differences in social behaviors between male and female animals, with males being more aggressive and less adult-oriented and females being more communicative, adult-oriented, and nurturing.[8] In humans as well, boys are, indeed, more inclined to rough-and-tumble play, while girls are more sedentary, more inclined to engage in grooming and nurturing forms of social engagement. Girls are also more inclined to seek adult attention and approval and imitate adult social behaviors, while boys tend to form groups independent from adult figures, even in preschool.[9] Boys use more imperative, directive language, while girls use more interrogative, reflective language.[10] Again this does not preclude some males from demonstrating a naturally more nurturing social style nor some females from being more aggressive than their peers. Given these data, however, there are at least some ways in which males and females differ from birth enough to warrant the application of different teaching methods.

Our schools, especially our public institutions, demand of all children at some point between the ages of four and seven that they sit at a desk and learn their letters, interact in groups in certain ways, and respond to adult direction with respect and obedience. Note that these are female-preferred early behaviors. At this juncture, it is

8. Molly R. Whitworth and Charles H. Southwick, "Sex differences in the ontogeny of social behavior in pikas: Possible relationships to dispersal and territoriality," *Behavioral Ecology and Sociobiology* 15 (1984): 175–82.

9. Eleanor E. Maccoby. "Gender and Relationships," *American Psychologist* 43 (April 1990): 513–20.

10. Ibid.

important to note, for later discussion, that more boys than girls are labeled by the schools as having behavioral disorders, learning disabilities, and attention deficits.[11] In reality, there are minor but significant differences between girls and boys from birth, which lead at least some of them to approach learning and social reality differently. The fact that the differences are minor and do not cause males and females to be grossly different in their interests and abilities in later life does not detract from the fact that there *are* differences and a good system of education will take them into account.

Individual Differences

It is established, then, that at least at some level, girls and boys are fundamentally different. It is also a basic axiom that within sexes, children are also different from one another, hence school-produced labels such as "gifted," "special," "learning disabled," and others. School and government policies maintain that all children are created equal, but the system spends millions of our dollars compensating for the fact that this is not the case. Within the average classroom, the fiction that all children, girls and boys, smart and less smart, handicapped and not handicapped, are the same, is maintained. The teacher has a lesson plan. He or she has a method. There is a corresponding set of homework assignments and tests. It is very interesting to note that on the one hand, all children are subjected to a basic set of lessons and corresponding work, whereas on the other hand children who fit some government definition of "special needs" are entitled to special treatment, to get them through the class work. To give credit appropriately, in some schools, children labeled "gifted" are also given special tasks to attempt to compensate for the inap-

11. American Psychiatric Association, *Diagnostic and Statistical Manual of Mental Disorders, Fourth Edition (DSM-IV)* (Washington, D.C.: American Psychiatric Association, 1994).

propriate pace of the classroom. Still others who do not fit the standard are given medications to get their behavior and style to conform to the classroom demands. Even given these minimal compromises with reality, the system neglects a basic fact—most traits exist on a continuum; from intelligence to temperament to learning styles, children are not all the same even after one removes those with extreme differences.

Children learn in different ways at different rates, not only based upon intelligence or early experience, or even sex, but also upon innate differences in style. This is one of the premises of the decades-old Montessori approach to learning, known for its consistent results at getting children, especially environmentally deprived children, to meet their potential and exceed predictions of their abilities. Some children are visual learners, others tactile, still others auditory. Some are more logical, others lean more toward intuitive ways of gaining knowledge. Further, they may take different approaches to different tasks.[12] These intellectual differences are not the only ones that may cause a child to fall away from the norm—some children are more active or more passive than others. Some are better at leading, others at following. These differences may change with age. Some children simply mature more slowly than others.[13] It is known that first-grade girls generally find it easier to sit in a first-grade seat for six hours than first-grade boys. Some children, regardless of gender, find sitting quietly more difficult than others even as they mature. Some children are active; others are sedentary. These differences are partly accounted for by sex differences and partly by temperamental differences, partly by physical differences, and partly by developmental differences. Rather than accept this situation and create an educational plan that accommodates basic differences, in our system all

12. Ricki Linksman, *How to Learn Anything Quickly* (Secaucus, N.J.: Carol Publishing, 1997).

13. Eileen M. Senior, "Learning disabled or merely mislabeled? The plight of the developmentally young child" 1986. *Childhood Education* 62 (1986): 161–65.

children are held to the same standard of "good behavior," the same standard of physical activity, the same standard of overall behavior. There are children who sit quietly better than others from an early age, and children who read sooner than others or do math sooner, just as at home we find children who walk earlier and talk earlier, grow teeth earlier, sleep through the night sooner. None of these basic differences in mental organization, temperament, and developmental rate is accounted for by standard school schedules and procedures. There is one basic set of expectations in any given classroom, which all children are expected to fulfill equally.

It is clear that children are not all on exactly the same developmental curve. Some walk sooner, some talk sooner, some crawl before they walk, others launch into running almost immediately. So what does the system do? It takes all children at or around a certain birthday and places them into a classroom with a predetermined set of demands and expectations. Some school districts offer a minor concession to individual differences and allow parents to choose when to place their children in first grade. Once they get there, however, the fact remains that they are again subjected to the same expectations as all the other children—active children, passive children, shy children, outgoing children, smart children, slow children, average children are all in the same classroom, placed into the same mold. This modern system of education bears resemblance to ancient systems where the bodies of children were warped to make them conform to some purpose: the "comprachicos" cruelly fitted children into jars and boxes to warp their bodies so that they would be fit only for slavery; in ancient China, the feet of girls were bound to cripple them and fit them only to be wives. In a supposedly more civilized way, modern pediatricians perpetuate the notion that children are the same—that every child must walk at a certain age or reach a certain weight by a certain time, supported by impressive charts of developmental milestones and growth percentiles that they hang on their office walls. The maintenance of the myth that all children actually are created equal begins with baby's first breath, when he is compared to other newborns, and so it goes. Our children are squeezed into the mold of the public schools from a very early age. Parents are convinced to cooperate with the demands of the schools regardless of their children's individual needs or interests or even abilities. The notion that all children must read at a given age has been institutionalized by schools and government; it has become a part of the very fabric of society. It will die hard.

It is a fact that all human beings are different from one another. Indeed, the world would quickly become monotonous if this were not the case. When government tries to educate masses of children, however, their individuality is sacrificed to the need for conformity and uniformity. This is no accident. It is a stated part of the goal of public schools to create good little worker-citizens—people who are long accustomed to an eight-hour workday and sedentary conditions, people who are used to following orders and behaving in a uniform, predictable way, people who know it is their purpose to fit in, to contribute to the common good.[14] Taking the magnificent variety of human children and forcing them all into jars of a similar size and shape, as the comprachicos did, does not fulfill the true purpose of education, the creation of minds ripe to take in and use information of many types, but instead a social purpose of sameness and conformity.

Square Pegs

What about the really nonuniform kids? The square pegs? The ones who are very smart or not too smart? The ones on the edges of the bell curve? What does a system designed with a "one size fits all" curriculum do with the odd-sized talents? It has been many years

14. Joel Spring, *Education and the Rise of the Corporate State* (Boston: Beacon Press, 1972).

since the passage of PL 94-142 in 1975[15] that schools have been under government mandates to provide special services to children labeled learning disabled, mentally handicapped, and the like, as well as children labeled "gifted." What exactly happens when the system tries to adjust without really changing, to fit those who are not actually "equal"?

A first attempt at making room for those who do not fit the round holes, particularly the slower children, was to isolate them into specialized classrooms. This worked so far as providing more tailored instruction, but it did not fulfill the real goal of a public school—to socialize the children into the real world. Thus was born "mainstreaming," mandated by PL 94-142 and applied in force in the early eighties. With mainstreaming, a child spends part of the day in a special environment structured to accommodate her physical, emotional, or cognitive needs, and the rest of the school day in a standard classroom. Now this is a *very* appealing idea on paper. Every child should grow up in reality—be with a variety of others, like him and unlike him, and learn to get along in the world with its varied demands. This

15. P.L. 94-142, The Education for All Handicapped Children Act of 1975 was passed in 1975. This law grew out of and strengthened earlier acts of a similar name, including P.L. 91-230 and P.L. 93-380. In summary, it proposes:

• To guarantee that a "free appropriate education," including special education and related service programming, is available to all children and youth with disabilities who require it.

• To ensure that the rights of children and youth with disabilities and their parents or guardians are protected (e.g., fairness, appropriateness, and due process in decision-making about providing special education and related services to children and youth with disabilities).

• To assess and ensure the effectiveness of special education at all levels of government. To financially assist the efforts of state and local governments in providing full educational opportunities to all children and youth with disabilities through the use of federal funds.

National Information Center for Children and Youth with Disabilites "The education of children with special needs: What do the laws say?" *NICHCY New Digest Interim Update*, Washington D.C.: National Information Center for Children and Youth with Disabilites (October 1996).

is true of the special-needs child as well as the child with more normative learning equipment. The reality is that the handicapped child remains handicapped when he enters the mainstream class. The results can be good or bad, but the process is far from simple. Many of these children require special aides to accompany them so that they can appreciate what transpires in the classroom. Others are simply not going to benefit regardless of special assistance, and the presence of extra adults in the room can be a distraction to the children not so accompanied.[16] It has also become standard for teachers to institute peer tutoring and group projects to accommodate special-needs children. The former provides the opportunity for the performance of a benevolent act on the part of the tutor as well as a chance for him to consolidate his knowledge, thus benefiting both students. The latter, in its common incarnation, is insidious: Children of higher and lower abilities work together for a single grade. There are only two possible outcomes here: Either the more-able children do all the work for the high grade they desire to achieve or the group genuinely works together, thus resulting in that socially desirable equalizing effect—at the expense of the grades of the better students in the group. Some cooperative learning experts have demonstrated academic as well as social benefits for both high- and low-ability students in groups,[17] but only given a specially developed curriculum, individual and group grades, and a school setting devoted to the concept of cooperative learning rather than as an add-on to conventional teacher-structured instruction.[18] Thus, given the current uses of group learning, the social goal of public education insis-

16. Robert E. Slavin, Nancy A. Madden, Nancy L. Karweit, et al., "Neverstreaming: Prevention and early intervention as an alternative to special education," *Journal of Learning Disabilities* 24 (1991): 373–78.

17. Robert E. Slavin, "Comprehensive Cooperative Learning Models," in Shlomo Sharan, ed., *Cooperative Learning* (New York: Praeger, 1990), pp. 261–83.

18. Shlomo Sharan, "Cooperative Learning: A Perspective on Research and Practice," in Sharan, *Cooperative Learning*, pp. 297–98.

tently rears its ugly head—equality and uniformity at the expense of fairness, in grades and educational opportunities as well as in economics. The parents who are footing the bill are entitled to ask, "Why does this child get more of our money spent on her education than my child? My child also has special needs." It is true, for no child is exactly the same as any other. Each is "special" in the true meaning of the word—distinctive and unique.

From another angle, take a brief peek at that *reality* for which that school is supposedly preparing those children. When they grow up and get jobs, their colleagues at the workplace are unlikely to be of one age or even one skill range. A classroom setting, however, confines them to a single age range. What if, instead of adding a handicapped six-year-old into a first-grade class full of six-year-olds, we took another cue from Montessori and placed all children of a certain level of ability into a single classroom? In a later section an example of a successful, ungraded secondary school not patterned on the Montessori method is discussed; this academic school resembles the swimming classes children attend at the local YMCA or, perhaps, a martial-arts class that relies on ability grouping regardless of age. There is clear precedent, both academic and nonacademic, for grouping children and other learners strictly by ability. In the profit-making world of swimming classes and martial arts and ballet, parents and students are inclined to take their tuition money elsewhere if students are not learning. Think of the financial incentives to the institution to make sure a given child is ready for the dance recital or passes that black-belt test. Public schools, however, are in no danger of losing their funding or their student bodies, thus preventing market incentives from operating on the most important schooling of all—the schooling of the minds of children.

There is another interesting difference between those athletic classes run by private organizations and those in the public schools—since there is no association between a certain age and a certain class (say the brown belt or the Junior Lifeguard)—individuals need not worry about how many times they must test before moving on! Thus the instructor can work with an individual on a certain skill or set of skills until the material is learned, with no stigma to the individual. He simply arrives at the next level when ready. As a corollary, if a given student is not achieving a given skill, one can look at the fit between teacher and the student and the student and the skill to see where the problem is, and solve it. If the teacher is not the right one for the student, a change can be made in this more flexible system. Alternatively, if the skill is one this student is simply unlikely to ever learn, she can be shifted onto a different learning track. Thus, the marketplace ensures not only accountability but also flexibility, which public schools deliberately avoid in their quest for equality.

Generally, it is acceptable to us that not every child is a gymnast or a swimmer. Once children have mastered basic skills relating to safety, most parents feel safe in allowing them to decide whether they would like to pursue a given course of instruction. With the training of their minds, however, we seem to insist that every child be a historian or a scientist, even beyond achieving basic understanding. Thus, in critiquing the current educational system, we must first agree upon what is meant by a basic education—a standard that nearly everyone can meet. It is easy to agree that all children who are able should learn to read, write, and do basic mathematical operations. We must also allow for individual differences in the rate and manner of achieving this basic standard. Not all children can learn these things by age six; not all children can learn to spell competently or perform algebraic functions. Given the spectrum of individual differences already discussed, an educational system that allows all children to pace themselves and maximize their achievement is the goal. Beyond that, we must take into account such phenomena as interest level and necessity when planning a more involved course of study. There must be a clear understanding of what a basic education represents and, once this is met, we must allow enough flexibility into the system that those children for whom more than the basics in mathematics or geography are not accessible or desirable get to expand their horizons in a different direction. With the positioning of the modern high school as a way station before college, the young student wishing to become an auto mechanic or a bartender or a shop owner has little incentive to take the process seriously.

Going to the other extreme, what of the children with higher learning potentials, those currently languishing under the euphemism "gifted"? In some schools, they are taken to a special classroom for an hour or so a day. They are segregated from their peers, made to stand out, and given extra work. Although it is certainly a benefit for a truly inspired learner to have an opportunity to go further, faster, a careful look at the basic structure of such programs belies their purpose. The children are generally not allowed to choose their enrichment activities. They are subjected, once again, to a standard, though ostensibly more advanced, curriculum. They are taken away from other classroom activities, which they are expected to fulfill in their free time. They are not given a higher set of expectations in the regular classroom from which they have been shifted for one brief hour—if everyone is writing the alphabet a hundred times to learn it, the gifted student who knew it two years ago is still writing. If everyone is doing fifty problems to be sure they can divide fractions, the gifted student who gets every one correct is expected to do all fifty. If the child should become bored and act out, she is punished rather than being given a more aptitude-appropriate task. How many novels have teachers taken from gifted students under the guise of discipline? Yet they complain that children have no love of reading. How many children are disciplined for reading ahead in a text they will have to read anyway, because they are bored of the classroom pace? But our children do not like to read, they tell us. What is the goal of this one-hour pullout program with its ensuing added homework load and the duplication of effort required for the child to catch up on the drudgery the other students perhaps needed to do while the gifted session was going on? How many of these children feel punished for being too smart, but continue to go just for the pleasure of being expected to learn something one hour a day or one hour a week, depending upon funding at the school? What school would get away with funding a program for its "special" students as stingily as for the "gifted"? Or not making accommodations in the classroom to be more in keeping with that child's ability? Gifted students do not receive classroom aides to push them beyond the expectations of the classroom.

There are many children, neither "gifted" nor "special," in every classroom, who are also not "average." They are unique. Does this rigid system adapt to their needs as individuals? Are there more math problems for those who have difficulty? Are there fewer problems for children who can demonstrate efficacy sooner? Is there a tactile teaching method offered to the tactile learners? Are active children allowed to move around as they learn? Are book reports assigned to children who hate to read differently than for avid readers? In the system as it exists now, the answers to the above questions remain "no." The system, despite limited compromises for those who do not fit their round holes, remains a "one size fits all" system. The children, however, are not all of one size.

Diagnosis: Wrong

Myriad differences in learning style have already been examined, but what of children who end up with the more damning labels our schools have the power to wield: learning disabled, attention deficit, behaviorally disordered? What do such labels actually mean? How valid is the application of such labels to school children? What is the effect of such labeling upon our children?

It is well known that attention-deficit disorder is the label of the decade. Five to six percent of children are estimated to have the constellation of behaviors labeled "attention-deficit hyperactivity disorder" (ADHD),[19] and far more demonstrate behaviors that lead to trips to the dean and the doctor at the bequest of teachers demanding certain standard classroom behavior. It turns out that the only way currently considered effective at achieving this uniformity of behavior among very active children, regardless of whether they truly fit the ADHD profile, is the administration of psychostimulant medication. Jokes are told about schools trucking in psychostimulants to feed to students at lunchtime. It is no joke, however, that millions of school children are on drugs—what is a joke is that while the government makes certain of them illegal, it makes others mandatory. All with the goal of standardizing the behavior of our children. Millions of school children are taking Ritalin[20] and other psychoactive drugs by prescription. Some of them have been diagnosed with attention-deficit hyperactivity disorder by qualified professionals; some of them have not. All of them are at risk from long-term use of psychoactive drugs. Already, there is a frightening implication that our children are being drugged more as a matter of control and compliance than anything one might rightfully call treatment.

What is ADHD and why does this label give schools a right to routinely medicate children? According to the *DSM-IV*—the diagnostic manual designated to be used by clinical and school psychologists in the diagnosing of mental disorders, ADHD represents a very specific set of symptoms. It is considered congenital, which means it is not, in the form designated in the manual, an acquired problem. Thus, diagnosis requires careful history-taking in addition to behavioral observations—except that the fine print in the *DSM-IV* also indicates that it might manifest in only two settings. The criteria require that the child must experience significant disturbance

---

19. Russell A. Barkley, *Attention Deficit Hyperactivity Disorder: A Handbook for Diagnosis and Treatment* (New York: Guilford Press, 1990), p. 63.

20. Mary Eberstadt, *Policy Review* 94 (April/May 1999), estimates that well over 3 million children are on Ritalin alone.

of functioning in those two settings.[21] The problem is obvious: disturbance as defined by whom? If a child is a problem to his teacher in the classroom and to the monitor on the playground, he may find himself on Ritalin, even if he is fine at home. The school, the ultimate authority on proper methods of child-rearing and appropriateness of behavior, is empowered by many parents to dictate medical and psychological treatments for their children. Indeed, many of these children who are seen as problem children in the school setting develop problem behaviors at home—but often only after the problems have begun in school. The assault on a child's fragile self-esteem of not being able to keep up with his peers, not being able to fill the expectations of authority figures, and not being able to behave as others seem able to do, is devastating. For many children labeled ADHD, it is uncertain which came first, serious problem behaviors or merely individual differences that were escalated by unrealistic demands.

In the case of ADHD, it is vital to examine the definition of "problem." As discussed above, some children are more active than others, some are more attentive. This is natural variation among individuals. Much has been written on the matter of whether ADHD is a real disorder, whether it is diagnosed too often, whether long-term medication is the appropriate treatment for even very young children. These are very important questions. In some ways, even professionals do not have the answers. We must keep asking, because our children are at risk. There are, without doubt, children who fit the criteria set forth in the *DSM-IV* for ADHD. They are, unquestionably, out of place in many classroom settings, especially the classrooms containing thirty chairs and thirty desks and thirty pairs of eyes belonging to thirty children of the same age but different abilities and interests, and one adult. They may even be difficult children at home: active, hypersensitive, loud, temperamental. But

21. *DSM-IV*, APA, 1994.

do they have a disorder? How do we distinguish between normal variants of behavior and actual psychological disorders, given the distortions of the expectations placed upon these children? As a Montessori teacher, this author came across only one child in four years in the classroom who would have fit the criteria for ADHD—one child out of approximately eighty. Not only is this significantly below the current estimates of prevalence of the disorder, it is also noteworthy that with certain accommodations, the child was able to function and learn within the environment provided, without medication.

Perhaps as important, does this diagnosable constellation of behaviors we call ADHD carry with it any adaptive potential? The author has worked professionally in several capacities—as classroom teacher, private tutor, and clinical psychologist, with individuals who fit the criteria for ADHD, both children and adults. There is no question that these individuals are different from the image the average family has of its little darling. But is it all bad news? These individuals tend to be very reactive to stimuli: *sensitive*. They tend to see life on a very short time line: *impatient*. They tend to think laterally rather than linearly: *creative*. They often act before thinking, following emotions rather than thoughts: *impulsive*. Perhaps the reader has already begun to see that this picture could be one of a problem child *or* of a potential great artist or inventor. It is all a matter of perspective, acceptance, and opportunity. There is reason to suspect that this group of symptoms or, more precisely, behaviors or traits, which we label ADHD, covaries with some adaptive functions. After all, evolution generally selects for traits with the potential for reproductive enhancement of the gene.[22] Just as the gene for sickle-cell anemia provides an adaptation that protects against malaria when carried singly, while creating disease only when paired, this set of behaviors

---

22. Randolph A. Nesse and George C. Williams, *Why We Get Sick: The New Science of Darwinian Medicine* (New York: Vintage Books, Random House, 1996).

labeled ADHD, which is so ill-suited for a modern classroom, may have been just the thing for inventing the wheel! Here is a glaring problem with the cookie-cutter our schools are applying to children— while they are selecting certain traits and behaviors to fit the mold, there remain other traits and behaviors that are part of the richness of human experience but are here being labeled "disorder."

There is no easy answer to the question of when we should diagnose impulsive/inattentive behavior as a disorder and apply medication. It is clear, however, that our social institutions are applying pressure to parents and children to attain a certain standard of behavior and that the application of these criteria is harmful to some children. What of a family with a child who fits the criteria for ADHD but chooses not to use medication? The child is at risk for more serious problems—social and educational—as she is likely to be disruptive in the classroom, scorned by peers, and fall behind academically. The family has few choices—though some choices do exist—for alternatives to the standard of treatment, the daily doses of psychostimulant medication. They can select another schooling option, they can select from a very few alternative treatment options, or they can basically cross their fingers, support each other, and help the child to cope. The system will press for that medication—it is easier. And they are right about that—it is far easier to medicate the unruly child and have the behaviors of concern drop away than to look further into the problem and seek a longer-term solution. It is evident that the alternatives are few and the demands of choosing among them high. What is a parent to do when a pediatrician, a principal, several teachers, and a school mental-health worker are all pressing for a certain outcome? What expert will she turn to after this barrage of professionals tells her she is harming her child by "withholding" treatment? The diagnosis of ADHD is likely to represent both a real constellation of behaviors and a phenomenon of the modern school that demands robotlike compliance with an ever-increasing series of demands and time constraints.

The label of "learning disabled" is also not without bite. Although it is certainly a more sophisicated and more accurate approach to admit that certain children learn more slowly or simply in a different way from others without being "stupid" or "ineducable," it is not necessarily an improvement to create a category of mental disorders, such as those found in the *DSM-IV*, to fit these differences. It is definitely not an improvement when the label of "learning disabled" is seen as a sign that there is something seriously wrong with the child. Contrary to public belief, having a learning disability does not mean a child reads backwards or has something seriously wrong with her. It means some aspect or aspects of her "processing circuitry," as it were, work differently from the anticipated way. Some children are simply unable to learn to read phonetically, lacking some aspect of the process that decodes symbols; woe to them in a system that teaches only phonics-based reading. Others are unable to sight-read due to some faulty memory process. How many such children were lost to the Dewey sight-reading craze? Reading is not the only process affected by learning problems. There can be specific inabilities to remember how to spell words, to do mathematical operations that involve arranging figures in space, to understand speech prosody, or expressiveness, or even to cope with certain social demands. Many of these glitches in the brain processes of children are not caught by school testing processes, which simply fail to detect these individuals. Children with such atypical learning problems may be thought of as lazy, underachieving, or unmotivated. After all, they appear as smart as the other students, but they are doing poorly in some or all of their academic work or they are getting on poorly with other children. Such children often fall through the cracks, becoming disruptive, depressed, unpopular, or enduring some other unpleasant result. The results are apt to linger into adulthood—turning children who did not fit into adults who cannot find their way in the world.

The other side of the learning disability coin is not much better. The children who are labeled, who are singled out as different so that they can be helped, are most frequently offered a slightly more intense version of just what they were doing in the regular classroom, because many schools simply do not have the resources for a thorough investigation of each child's individual learning style. *Children are individuals.* This cannot be stressed enough. Even a child with a specific dyslexia, who cannot sight-read, may learn better with auditory input versus visual input or sensory input versus auditory input. Learning disabilities are real and represent real flaws or variants in the information-processing system, but they need not be sentences of lifelong illiteracy and ignorance and low self-esteem. Most individuals can be taught to cope with their individual differences and achieve a good outcome, learning enough to get along in the world and finding ways to develop difference into distinction and failure into success, though the outcome may not fit the mold offered by the public school system. Parents, in their naïve assumption that the schools know best, as well as their disadvantaged state of having given heavily in taxes with no resources left to pay for additional educational assistance, are often paralyzed in their need to do something for their children. They may believe that there are no other options; they may believe that there is nothing more they can do, and worse, they may believe that there is something really wrong with their children.

Schools also label some of their charges as behavior problems. We all know who they are supposed to be: the bullies, the kids who set fires, the kids who are always truant or on drugs. Many districts have special classrooms or special schools for such children; others do not. But how many are asking the hard question: For those with genuine school-related behavior disorders, should this child be in school at all? Especially for the younger students, this question is never asked until the district throws its figurative hands up in disgust and expels the child. It is a source of endless fascination to this writer that whereas every child supposedly has a right to a certain minimal education, the system has some contradictory right to give up if the task is too difficult. Even preteens fall between the cracks, either being expelled at a young age or simply pushed through the system to fulfill the mandate, but without the system's actually being accountable for the child's progress.

Moving from the young, unruly children to the teens they become, is anything the system does to force this child to remain in school actually going to cause learning to occur? What options are there for such children *before* they wind up in jail? There was a story years back about a town in Texas which, in its infinite governmental wisdom, was taking driving licenses from teens who dropped out of school before a certain age. To some, this has a certain logic—they must go to school or do nothing. From another perspective, a more individual-friendly approach, we can see that these youths might have gone on to have jobs and become productive, even if at a lower than optimal status, if allowed their transportation. This is a similar type of wisdom to the suspension. The students most likely to get suspended are the ones who do not want to be in school for some reason. They are disruptive, they cut classes, they are truant, they do drugs or smoke on campus. When they are punished by suspending them from class, it is the system that is confused—that's what such students want—to be out of school. Long ago, Maria Montessori offered the wisdom that the high school is not the ideal learning environment for teenagers.[23] This is hardly a universally held truth, but it is obvious that there are glaring problems with American secondary education. When we are reduced to having school hallways patrolled to keep students in, when we are having to patrol the grounds to send them back, when we are having to enforce broad, damaging punishments upon them and their families to keep them returning, and when schools become focal points of extreme and

23. Maria Montessori, *From Childhood to Adolescence* (New York: Schocken Books, 1973).

violent behaviors, then we must look at the system, not the children, for the problem.

Teachers complain yearly that they are spending more time disciplining students than teaching students. What if we admit that adolescents need something more than intellectual pursuits? That they need time to experience the real world, to develop marketable skills, to understand their changing needs? What if we open the system to variability? Allow parents and students to share in decisions about how, when, and how much is the appropriate education for a given teen? Who is the beneficiary of this structure? Only the system—the bureaucracy that is perpetuating a system which fails to address the needs of many if not most of those it purports to serve. On the heels of the terrible events in Littleton, Colorado, in 1999, where two such unruly teens wantonly slaughtered their schoolmates, we must also look at the fact that the measures being taken in modern high schools to ensure safety, gestures that were nonexistent twenty years ago, fail to solve the problem of students going out of control.

EXAMPLES: WHAT CAN WE LEARN?

The Ultimate Cookie-Cutter: Japanese Education

The Japanese model of education has long been held up to the United States as a paragon of educational excellence: a precise, regimented, rigorous system in which everyone participates and everyone achieves certain minimal standards. We are told to look at the numbers of scientists and mathematicians coming out of that system and work to model our own more along the lines taken by the Japanese. There are reasons, however, why we cannot and should not attempt to emulate the Japanese educational system.

The United States is not Japan. Our country lacks the rigid behavioral customs historically and culturally entrenched in Japanese society. Our country lacks the cultural and racial homogeneity of Japan, which remains ninety-nine percent native Japanese. Our society lacks the tightly constrained social structure in which an individual with a certain level of education enters the job market at a certain level, essentially with his stable and predictable future decided for him. The United States cannot hope to re-create a system that has been developed over centuries in such a different cultural milieu.

Additionally, although the Japanese system may, indeed, produce some superior training for many people, it is hardly a paragon of educational success. Japanese primary education is arguably superior in absolute amount of knowledge imparted, but cultural differences make it difficult to translate Japanese methods into U.S. schools.[24] What might be learned from the Japanese is that research into what works is a valuable place to invest time and money.[25] More important, what should *not* be learned from Japan is what occurs beyond the primary grades.

In Japan, most secondary students spend countless after-school hours in juku, special examination preparatory schools, in order to pass exams to qualify for high school or college, indicating that the many hours they spend in school—many more hours than our children—fail to prepare them for the expectations at the next level.[26] The rigid Japanese system also produces a high rate of low self-esteem, depression, and suicide among young people, which, although lower than the rate in America, is alarming to the Japanese, traditionally a peaceful people.[27] The last and perhaps most important

24. Harold W. Stevenson and James W. Stigler, *The Learning Gap* (New York: Summit Books, 1992), pp. 7–11.

25. Ibid., p. 23.

26. Yoshio Sugimoto, *An Introduction to Japanese Society* (Cambridge, U.K.: Cambridge University, 1997), p. 112.

27. Jon Woronoff, *The Japanese Social Crisis* (New York: St. Martin's, 1997), pp. 215–23.

difference is that the Japanese system, with its culturally pro-grammed, carefully regimented, extremely demanding structure, is designed to weed out the individual, to discourage independent thinking, and to eliminate the very differences that give our society its richness and flavor. Japanese teachers are discouraged from ex-pressing creativity in their approach to teaching and the students only rarely are seen to discover their own creativity.[28] Japan is a highly homogeneous country, whereas the very founding of our country contained the premise that there is richness in diversity. The Japa-nese system not only will not work here, but it is barely working in Japan in today's demanding, international society.

What of violence in the Japanese model? In addition to being depicted as a model of rigorous and successful education, Japan is held out as a paragon of the gunless, nonviolent society. Japanese students, however, increasingly engage in a form of collective bullying so prevalent that it has been given a name: *ijime*.[29] Additionally, it appears that even as those who would blame guns for the behavior of people are calling for stricter gun control in light of a series of terrible incidents in our public schools, Japan's incidence of school violence is also at an all-time high. Students do not have access to guns in Japan; they are using knives and other weapons.[30] It is time to look beyond the obvious scapegoat of the weapon to the reality that school children are being put under enormous pressure. In Japan, the pressure is to fit precisely into a system with no room for deviation. In the United States, the pressures are similar, despite a very different cultural basis. Conformity is demanded of youths at a time when, biologically and developmentally, they are discovering their individuality, and, in the United States, in a nation thats lacks the cultural uniformity of Japan, a country where diversity is an

28. David Suzuki and Keibo Oiwa, *The Japan We Never Knew* (Toronto, Canada: Stoddart, 1996), pp. 289–303.

29. Sugimoto, *Japanese Society*, pp. 127–28.

30. *Japan Echo* 25, no. 3 (June 1998).

inescapable, visible fact of life. Indeed, there is much to be learned, but not to emulate, in the Japanese system.

A Nongraded High School

A nongraded high school created in Florida in 1958 has something more relevant to offer to American schools. Much like the nonacademic classes discussed earlier, Melbourne High School was restructured to classify students according to achievement rather than age and to promote them according to learning accomplished rather than time of year. When tested for ability grouping, the students who had once occupied the same age-grouped classroom were as much as ten years apart in language skills. The range of mathematical skill was greater still.[31]

A second discovery in the process of ungrading was that many entering students lacked the basic skills and knowledge required for high school courses. Given the skill-based system, these students were allowed all the time and given all the help they needed to achieve basic competencies in language and mathematics. No stigma was attached to their plight, and no higher standard demanded of them until they were ready. No lower or upper limit was enforced; the expectation was that each student would achieve his or her potential, and the opportunity was provided for them to do so.[32] One might worry that achievement would lag in such a setting, but the result was the opposite: students in the ungraded setting, compared with children in comparable graded settings, achieved higher average scores on achievement tests.[33]

A final relevant difference between Melbourne High School and the typical American public high school: teachers are positioned as

31. B. Frank Brown, *The Nongraded School* (Englewood Cliffs, N.J.: Prentice-Hall, 1963), p. 49.
32. Ibid., p. 53.
33. Ibid., p. 189–99.

"removers of roadblocks"[34] rather than founts of knowledge. The assumption in this environment, as in the Montessori environment discussed earlier, is that children learn by nature. The best we can offer them is advice on how to learn and what to learn and where to find it. Information can be located, given the proper tools; critical thinking and free inquiry must be modeled, not taught.

From this brief peek at ungraded schooling, we learn that it is possible to create a less rigid system of mass education and produce an acceptable end result: educated individuals. This particular structure is only one possibility. The more important lesson, however, is that the rigid mold into which current U.S. public education forces children, and the even stricter mold into which Japanese students are forced, is not essential to mass education. If education is indeed the goal, rigid molds are, in fact, detrimental.

MORE IS BETTER: A TALE OF TIME AND MONEY

The "more is better" approach is common to government projects. If mind-altering drugs are bad, then regulating them is good, and the more laws there are, the better, despite evidence that the original set did not have the desired effect of reducing drug use. If guns are bad and gun control is good, regardless of the fact that some gun control is not working to reduce gun-related crime, more anti-gun laws will do the job. Thomas Sowell calls this "The Vision of the Anointed,"[35] the "socially responsible" logic of politicians and bureaucrats which is impervious to facts and clear evidence. The "more is better" hypothesis is applied in at least two separate ways to schools: More time is better, and more money is better. There are fallacies within each of these assumptions.

34. Ibid., p. 147.
35. Thomas Sowell, *The Vision of the Anointed* (New York: Basic Books, 1995).

Days of Our Children's Lives

School takes up more of our children's lives every year, and legislation is proposed at the local, state, and national levels every year to enable it to take even more. The logic is that since education is good on principle, and schooling is the way to create education, more schooling will necessarily create more education. Thus it follows in current logic that, in light of the evidence that education is not consistently occurring, more schooling should succeed where less has failed. These premises are false. Mowing the lawn is good for it on principle, but if we continue to cut it shorter and shorter because it looks brown, its health is unlikely to improve. Rather than continuing to run the mower futilely, we must look for another need of the lawn that has not been filled. With increasing demands on our children's time by public schools, educational outcome, as determined by literacy and test scores, has not improved. What else do they need?

Project Head Start was founded on the premise that early childhood deprivation could lead to poor school performance. Considering the huge corpus of research indicating that even rats are made smarter by enriched early environments[36] and the wonderful work done by Maria Montessori in Italian ghettos in the late 1800s demonstrating that deprived children could outperfom nondeprived children if given early enrichment,[37] there is nothing faulty with the assumption that enrichment will help children to adapt better to school and make more of their potential. What is wrong with this assumption is the corollary that appears to have been added sans research—that more school is always better. It is crucial to examine this assumption thoroughly, as it is part of the vision with which

36. P. A. Dell and F. David Rose, "The impairing effect of environmental impoverishment in rats: A cognitive deficit?" *IRCS Medical Science: Psychology & Psychiatry* 14 (1986): 19–20.

37. Maria Montessori, *The Discovery of the Child* (Madras, India: Kalakshetra Publications, 1948).

government extracts more and more time from the lives of our children.

Did Project Head Start, the first test of the "more is better" assumption, fulfill its promise? Was taking underprivileged children out of their homes at earlier ages the key to success in later schooling? As it turns out, the results were mixed. In very early school experience, the children selected for such programs did indeed fare better than their peers, scoring better on tests and doing better in school—but the results were short-lived. Later testing indicated a leveling-off effect. Head Start may have given its beneficiaries a boost in early learning and a better attitude toward schooling, but without changes at every level, the cognitive advantage was soon lost.[38]

Without data to support such decisions, one result of the assumption that more is better with regard to school is that many locales are attempting to make kindergarten mandatory. Other areas have established year-round schooling, and yet others have created longer school days. In other words, since Head Start gave a degree of legitimacy to the assumption that more is better, regardless of actual data, the results of that assumption are becoming part of the entrenched wisdom of the system. There is no research data to support the continual adding of time to the mandatory school sentence, but legislatures continue to put forth proposals that begin with the assumption that what is wrong with the system can be fixed by doing more of it.

Perhaps a more prevalent result of the "more is better" assumption is that many parents, naively assuming that the professional educators and lawmakers know what is best, tolerate outrages such as holidays being removed from the school calendar or school being extended into the summer season to make up for "snow days," on the premise that hours spent in school are irreplaceable. Every school child knows

38. Ron Haskins, "Beyond Metaphor: The Efficacy of Early Childhood Education," *American Psychologist* 44 (1989): 274–82

that this is silly. First, when holidays are taken from children, they are unlikely to be cooperative students on the days they spend at a desk instead of playing. Second, when holidays are taken from teachers, they are unlikely to have lesson plans developed to compensate for the transference of school days from early in the year to later in the year, and, indeed, even they are likely to harbor some resentment at being in the classroom when they had the expectation of being elsewhere on that day. One commonplace result of the "more is better" assumption, then, is that children sit in schools for a legislatively mandated number of hours per week and days per year regardless of whether actual learning is occurring during any given hour or day.

The consequences of creating a rigidly structured system that correlates how much is learned with how many hours are spent in school reach into the life of the family. How many families must make difficult choices—made difficult, mind you, by the mistaken belief that legislators know what is best in the realm of education— to have one child who may be in a different school, out on vacation while the other is in, or to have the parents off work on the holiday that the children are spending in school? It appears that the "more is better" assumption carries with it a corollary assumption that *less* time with family is not bad! Thus, our federal and state governments run up against a contradiction of their own creation: They espouse both the idea that more time is needed in the classroom and the idea that families should spend more time together. While government officials are heard bemoaning the fate of the family in America, it is government policies that are separating children from their homes earlier and earlier, for more and more hours and days, and forcing two parents to work to make enough money to support these interventive programs.

There are even more negative effects of the "more is better" assumption: Parents, trusting an educational system that has, after all, the benefit of experience and superior wisdom about such things, begin to doubt their ability to teach their own children. After all, how can one or two parents who have jobs, a home to care for, nurturance responsibilities toward one or more children, and countless other demands on their time, teach children, especially if the professionals are struggling with the task? Of course, to some, since there is a huge system, for which they are already paying exorbitant amounts of money, already in place, why, indeed, should they take the time to learn to do such a thing? It is essentially already a fait accompli. Indeed, why would one undertake a task that, it has been decided by wiser heads, should be the responsibility of society? What an inordinate time commitment must be required, if one looks at the time, money, and energy the schools put into the project!

Parents by and large surrender to inertia, to the knowledge that the horrific task of educating their children and, with it, the responsibility for the project, has been lifted from them. Whew! They heave collective sighs of relief. In leading an examined life, however, it is important to check each premise upon which we base our decisions, whether the default decision to do what is expected, or the more risky decision to take an alternate path. We will look first at the time-usage assumption. Children spend about six hours a day, five days a week, forty weeks a year in school. If an individual parent, who still had other responsibilities, were to make this sort of commitment, it would be Herculean. Looking at the actual time spent in the process of education during those legislature-mandated hours, however, it quickly becomes evident that the requirement is much less in an individual household, for an individual child or a small number of children.

To begin, schools have to meet a certain set of requirements about saying the Pledge of Allegiance and singing patriotic songs. They have to take attendance. There are announcements and administrative tasks to complete even before the ostensible task of teaching is allowed to begin. Generous figures place this at between one and two hours a day. Now our home school or private school is down to four or five hours, because it doesn't have to do these things. The public school teacher is faced with twenty to thirty children of the same age, but different patience levels, different learning aptitudes, different backgrounds, and different personal styles. But there is only one classroom, one gym, one playground, one schedule, which all must follow—sometimes even with regard to bathroom breaks! At home, parents have one or a few children. Even with the worst possible variance in ages and temperaments, individualized attention can be given to each and energy spent on discipline is minimized. With the smaller numbers, it is not destructive to the process of education if one child is running around in the backyard while others are reading quietly and others are making cookies! Thus children can, indeed, be working in their best modality, moving with their own individual needs and rhythms, and the parent-teacher can even be assumed to get something of his or her own done in this time, perhaps even paid at-home work, as the author did. Private schools obviously operate with more constraints than home schools, but even then, with fewer bureaucratic demands and more control over the demeanor of the pupils, time demands for activities other than teaching are minimized.

Just how many daily hours would we assume it takes to educate a few children versus many children with an individualized curriculum versus a single curriculum? How much "homework" is our home-taught child given? How much is the private school pupil assigned? What, exactly, is the difference in scheduling learning into those five or fewer hours? To begin, looking into the classroom, it is evident that even in a graded classroom where fast learners have been separated from slow learners, there are still twenty to thirty individual children awaiting education. Factoring in time for questions from each, the fact that there will be some who never understand a word of a given lecture, the fact that there are some who are visual learners and never heed a word of that lecture, and the fact that there are still others who are reading Judy Blume, a teacher in a public classroom has a lot to achieve in a class period. In an individualized setting, by contrast, there may be no lecture—rather individualized explanations or demonstrations, after which questions can be asked and learning clarified. In the public setting, the homework is also "one size fits all"; the whole class is given an assignment that some may do easily, some may do competently, and others may find quite challenging. In the individualized setting, the assignments can be tailored to the learner: One child may need no additional work on an assignment to master the material, while another needs to practice, and still another needs more instruction and even more practice.

In practical terms, what this means is that, in the nonpublic setting, any given child need not spend time sitting though a lecture he is incapable of comprehending or a lecture of which she has no need. Assignments tailored to the student are vastly more efficient and can be significantly shorter—allowing a child to practice skills he finds difficult and to move ahead when ready. Individualized education allows each child to proceed at her own pace and not to spin her wheels on material that she is never going to learn at all. Homeschoolers find that an hour or two a day suffices even for large families, at the elementary level. At the high school level, perhaps twice as much time is required to allow for more detailed knowledge, more complex problems, and more demanding writing assignments. In the home school, time is not devoted exclusively to paper-and-pencil tasks but to a variety of learning and enrichment experiences, as well as maintaining the home itself. Private schools often have the same experience, that formal lessons can be confined to a few hours a day, and the balance of time can be allotted for individual projects or enrichment experiences. The bottom line in the allocation of time to education is that when students are allowed to work within their competence, to follow their interests, and when teachers are exclusively interested in imparting knowledge and encouraging learning, rather than creating conformity and regimentation, education is not a very time-intense project; neither does it demand full-time, exclusive adult attention. Again, the "more is better" assumption suffers from real-life experience in nontraditional learning environments.

Significantly, the "more is better" assumption starts from the assumptions that all children are created equal and that all teaching is equally effective and that all work is equally valid for all students. If this were true, perhaps more of the same would indeed offer more benefits; but since it is false, just having children present for more hours is unlikely to get them better educated. More time does, however, allow for more social control of children and less parental influence.

Good Money after Bad

The "more is better" assumption is also applied to the financial aspect of the public school morass. The assumption states that if $5,000 a year fails to educate students, then $10,000 will succeed. If one computer in a school fails to educate students, then one in every classroom will succeed. If one teacher to thirty students fails to achieve education, then one to twenty-nine will succeed. Taxpayers are made to dip more deeply into their pockets yearly for the education of children. The "more is better" assumption carries with it the message that if education is not happening, spending more money will automatically cause it to happen. It doesn't matter so much how this money is spent, just that it is made available to educators. Some favor smaller class sizes, some more special services, others more field trips, and yet others better buildings. There is even one local district that has allocated money to loan every student in its high school a laptop computer for the duration of their enrollment! There is certainly no limit to how many different ways money can be spent on the education of children. Many of these ideas have validity—but they are not working!

In reality, it is neither difficult nor expensive to educate children. Given community resources such as libraries and museums, given certain basics such as books and paper and, perhaps, taking advantage of modern conveniences, such as a computer with internet access, whether at home or at a local library, the home-based education of a child is a very low-budget project. For example, history textbooks can cost as much as $100 each, but primary and secondary source material can be found at a library or even on the internet, a resource that can be accessed at most libraries, and learning can be dramatically enhanced by students having to decide issues of right and wrong rather than having these fed to them, predigested by textbook authors. Thus, at no cost beyond a contribution to the library, whether voluntary or tax-based, students can avail themselves of all that they need to gain a solid working knowledge of history. What about mathematics? Again, though a textbook is a useful tool in this case, structuring and organizing learning, it does not have to be purchased. Instead, it can be borrowed from a library or rented short-term, learned from, and returned. Alternatively, groups of problems can be sent to students over the internet or in the mail for solving, with solutions and explications provided later. Most important, though, in the home school students learn how to learn and where to find information. A formal school setting requires more organization and setup, more space and supplies, but it is not the sophistication of the materials or the cost of the facility that creates education. Education occurs in the interface between mind and experience, and there are many means to that end. It immediately becomes clear that the big costs of public schools are not in the learning materials themselves, but in the maintenance and building of physical plants, in the salaries of teachers, the support staff, and the huge bureaucracy that administers all these layers. In fact, with the rise of mass education, as the number of students has increased, the number of teachers has increased less dramatically than the number of administrators.[39] Thus, the ineffective education dollar has to cover a good deal more than the process of teaching children.

39. Randall Collins, *The Credential Society* (Orlando, Fla.: Academic Press, 1979), p. 117.

If more is better when it comes to spending money on education, then why do homeschoolers do so well, coming from learning environments in which little money is spent? The reality is that the magnitude of the project is what costs money, not the process of education itself. When society tries to educate children in uniform groups with the demands for certain behaviors, certain rates of learning, certain production of work, certain length of school term, need is created for a structure with which to ensure the entirety of this process. The current structure, with its corresponding rigidity and bureaucracy, emerged gradually throughout the first half of the twentieth century. Before that, children were not simply placed in grades by age or promoted regardless of achievement, nor were there huge bureaucracies creating evermore rigidity. Were the goal exclusively education, then the project would have remained smaller. When society overlaid the demand for conformity and uniformity and social goals on top of goals of actual literacy and competence, then a different demand was set up, with a correspondingly different set of costs. Illinois high schools spend an average of $10,019 per student yearly.[40] The author, with three children currently in these institutions, contributes $1,200 annually in property taxes to high schools, $1,600 to grammar schools, and $120 to the local college. Given the return of this $2,920, the author is certain she could adequately provide educational experiences for three teenagers, as was the case several years ago when all three were homeschooled, at a cost in the purchase of books and the taking of trips to museums and the like, of less than $2,000 yearly for all three. In fact, homeschooling is currently estimated to cost $546 per child out of pocket.[41] Looking again at the private market-based system within which many children

40. Glenbard Township District 87 Community Relations Office, "Glenbard West High School 1998 School Report Card" (Glen Ellyn, Ill.: Glenbard Township District 87 Community Relations Office, October 1998).

41. Brian D. Ray, "Nationwide Study" (Salem, Ore.: National Home Education Research Institute, June 1997).

learn gymnastics and ballet, local charges average $5 per hour for instruction in various class sizes with varied needs for expensive equipment and facilities. At $10,000 per student, given the approximately 1,000-hour school year, the cost per hour for public school education is about $10 per hour. It is the cheaper, nonacademic, non-age-graded, market-based systems that produce the more reliable results.

It takes more than money to produce education. It takes willingness to learn on the part of the students and knowledge of how to produce desired results on the part of the teachers. It takes flexibility within a system such that different children can be treated as individuals toward the goal of achieving those results. More money does not buy more education. Appropriate goals, relating strictly to academic as opposed to social goals, individualized lessons, and achievement-based placement, are more likely to have the desired result. The gymnastics class is not trying to make its students into citizens, nor is it trying to make them all the same—it is trying to teach them gymnastics. The karate school is not trying to make students into citizens—it is trying to teach them karate. Both of these examples represent skills that require a great deal of discipline on the part of students to achieve progress, but it is rare that a gymnastics coach or sensei spends an entire class period disciplining students. It is unheard of for these professionals to need instruction in maintaining discipline. The discipline is built into the process—it is a natural part of the demand of the situation, and the pupils, who are there willingly, cooperate. If students were not learning karate, would we simply build a bigger dojo or find a more costly instructor? No, but we would take our karate-lesson dollars elsewhere. The amount of money is not the issue. The market process by which consumers get what they pay for and pay for what they want to get is a significant missing ingredient in public schooling.

Schools yearly call for more tax money—to purchase computers, to repair buildings, to hire more teachers or administrators, to purchase new equipment or textbooks, to perform research into why children fail to learn, to give more tests demonstrating pupil efficacy. The trend continues: However much money is spent, more is always demanded, and the bottom line, educational failure, although it may rise and fall, rarely changes substantially. Many, many children fail to achieve minimal literacy in public schools. Many others drop out. Still others leave believing there is something wrong with them that they could not meet the goals set forth by the system. Others leave full of medication with dire predictions about their futures. More tax dollars do not produce the goal of better education, nor do more tax dollars make children all alike. No amount of money will make a "one size fits all" system adaptive to individual needs.

TEACHERS

The argument is heard in myriad guises that children must be in school, that school is the only place where they can be educated, and that only properly trained professionals can educate. This is an odd sort of package deal. Years before there were any public schools, people still learned. Long before they attend any school at all, children learn. Maria Montessori's entire system of education was based on the premise that the inner drive of the child is to learn, to become a "man." What sort of miracle must it be that children learn to talk, to use the complex symbols of language, without benefit of a certified teacher? What are these magic teachings imparted to students in schools of education to which no one else has access? What is the special magic of legislative bodies that they can *know* what makes a good teacher and enforce their superior wisdom upon teacher-training programs?

This author once had an enlightening conversation with the head of the Illinois legislative committee in charge of education. Having received several phoned pleas from schools desperate for a teacher capable of providing services to homebound students, this author set about determining what credentials would be needed to begin work. Already equipped with a substitute teaching certificate, a job grading essays for several local schools, a B.A. in English, and a certification in Montessori education, having already owned and operated a school, having begun master's level work in family studies, the writer was confident that a mere rubber stamp was in order, especially considering the desperation of the need in the local schools. After a careful look at the proffered credentials, the legislator scoffed, "But you lack a class in speech and a class in mainstreaming handicapped children." "But why," opined the author, "should I need a class in speech when I have a B.A. in English language and literature from a highly prestigious university?" "Because it is in the law." "And why," she continued, "should I need a class in mainstreaming handicapped children when I am not to be in a classroom setting, especially considering that I am already in the classroom setting when I work as a substitute?" "Because in their wisdom, the legislators have decreed that that is what is required of a teacher." "And how," continued the author, "can we expedite this process to get immediate assistance to these students who are currently without a teacher?" Needless to say, the rest of the conversation went around the same tree with the result that the children whose needs were to have been met by the author's appearance on the scene went without services.

We have teachers' colleges and student teaching experience and we have legislative mandates for what is to be taught. In some states, we have the additional overlay of state qualifying examinations for teachers. None of these processes, however, face the real question of what makes a good teacher. The author submits that it is not teachers' college that makes a good teacher, but some intangible ability to impart information. It is likely to be true that some aspects of this ability can be quantified and taught, but it is by no means as easy as going to a certain school and taking certain classes. Additionally, when we look at the course of study prescribed for future teachers, we see a large number of administrative and management and discipline-related courses and a relative dearth of content courses and courses on child psychology and theories of learning. The individuals teaching physics at a high school level are not professional physicists with a penchant for teaching, but teachers, trained in the methods legislatures have deemed appropriate to fulfill a particular agenda related to public schooling, and a course or two in physics. The difference is significant. Not only is it the difference between book-learning and practical applications, but the difference between schooling and educating.

In a teachers' college, prospective teachers learn to manage a classroom, administer tests, and discipline students. They learn to follow a curriculum and create a lesson plan. Where does one learn how to reach another mind? How to offer information in different ways for different students? How to keep the interest of each and accommodate the needs of each? This is a thing more elusive. The curriculum dictates that a certain measure of learning must go into each student and that each student must be graded based on her ability to demonstrate having achieved knowledge. Who is grading the teacher's ability to impart this knowledge? Having achieved employment and then tenure, the teacher is a fixture, and the student is the one who has to succeed! A very strange circumstance indeed from a business perspective. Regardless of the teacher's skill at teaching, students pass or fail based on some supposedly objective standard meant to represent the achievement of knowledge. In this way, every failure by a teacher to produce learning is passed on to students.

The bureaucratic structure of this system, firmly entrenched by the teacher's unions and the government, resists attempts to review, revise, or repair. Qualifying exams fail to disqualify. This author was once hired to train a young teachers' college graduate for the state qualifying examination in English, which she had failed on her first attempt. The young woman, diploma in hand, was unable to read more than rudimentary material, could not distinguish homophones, and had no rules in place in her head for using punctuation. She is

currently teaching biology to students somewhere in Illinois. Qualifying examinations and periodic reviews fail to produce change.
Union rules ensure that this is the case. The system is carefully
constructed to prevent change—but among parents and even politicians who can see the statistics clearly informing them that education is failing to occur in today's public schools, there is mounting
outcry for change.

Another recent and disturbing phenomenon has been observed
repeatedly by the author in the local public elementary schools: envy
or, perhaps, resentment, not of one pupil for another, but of teachers
for gifted students. The author recalls a time when gifted students
were called "teacher's pet" and treated with disdain by their class-
mates. However, in the new school environment, it is often the
teachers who are subjecting gifted students to negative differential
treatment. The author has observed several dramatic examples of
such behavior in two local schools, in one case resulting in the parents
withdrawing the child from school entirely. Teachers have been observed to refuse to accept regular classroom assignments from students who have been pulled out for gifted enrichment programs.
They have been observed to refuse to give credit on tests for correct,
but non-rote responses to short-answer questions. They have been
observed to concoct reasons for lowering the grades of gifted students
by such means as accusing such students of cheating or by losing the
students' assignments. Student envy was a negative trend of public
schools from early days, this newer phenomenon of teachers envying
or resenting their students is new and treacherous.

The author suggests that this frightening and destructive trend
stems from many sources. It may relate to the lower standards for
providing credentials to teachers as well as the increased difficulty
of releasing incompetent or destructive individuals from their jobs.
It may also relate to the frustration and helplessness experienced by
teachers. Today's teachers are being asked to do the impossible: teach
the same curriculum in the same way to huge numbers of children

each of whom is different from the others, give myriad tests to prove that learning has occurred while still finishing the year's lesson plans, and maintain order in classrooms in which discipline has long since become a moot point—where teachers may indeed fear for their safety. Perhaps the gifted student is too much of a challenge for these highly distressed individuals.

One of the suggestions that has begun to achieve public support and even trials in select areas of the country is that of having professionals who actually have working knowledge of the subject matter teach upper-level students about highly specific areas such as physics and chemistry. What would happen if scientists or other professionals, with book knowledge as well as real-world experience, taught children? "But how would the system ensure education if there were no standards?" ask those seeking to maintain the status quo. Here we have come full circle—children and youths learned long before there were teachers' colleges. They learned naturalistically, in the home, how to walk and talk and cook and hunt. They learned from the environment—again, a principle expounded by Maria Montessori a century ago. They took apprenticeships and learned while doing. They learned many things in many modalities. And there were people who were teachers—whose vocation was to impart knowledge. But this was not sacred; learning was expected to occur in the world, via exposure to many places, many people, many experiences. All people learn daily, but for children, learning is their way of life. It cannot be stopped, though it can certainly be catalyzed, facilitated, enhanced or, sadly, discouraged. It is important that our children are kept safe and given the best opportunities to learn as much as they can, but it is in no way inevitable that there is only one right way for this to occur or one right type of person to ease the process along. Not only is there not only one way to train teachers, there is no one right sort of person suited to be a teacher—learners and teachers need to be able to work cooperatively to the benefit of each. In the system as it now exists, however, the irrational belief that only a state can determine who should teach children has become sacred.

TAXATION, TAX CREDITS, VOUCHERS, AND CHOICES

Sacred also are the schools themselves: the idea that all children should be educated and that all working adults should help to foot the bill. Even the most strenuous objectors to mandatory education are liable to come out in favor of vouchers or tax credits. After all, everyone knows that education is a value shared by all members of society, so they should all be equally willing to pay for the schooling of children, theirs or otherwise. If the situation could be improved upon, so that parents and students had more choice, more control, certainly this would provide for better outcomes. It is agreed by those who believe in free markets that competition would enhance the business of providing education. This may not be clear to all, but it is a relatively safe assumption. However, the next step is less clear. The usual arguments go one of two ways: either that government should continue to collect money and redistribute it based more upon parents' choices in the education of their children, or that government should get out of the education business and allow the market to provide options and price variety and satisfy other as yet unthought-of demands of a market in education. Many thinkers and even some politicians believe that tax credits or vouchers represent effective ways to encourage a freer marketplace in education, forcing schools to be accountable for the results they produce, while giving parents more latitude and control in the education of their children. Others will insist that this is but a bandage over a gushing wound, that the system cannot be fixed, and that the stopgap measures being proposed have the potential to make the situation worse.

The first problem, of course, is the assumption that schools are some sort of public commodity for which all should pay. This assumption apparently arises from two beliefs. The first is that children would universally be illiterate if parents were not forced to send them to school and if school were not "free." The second is that the education of youth is somehow a public good, a product from which all benefit equally in the long run. The first assumption is easily challenged. As described above, children learn. It is what they do. Children learned long before public schools existed, and they will continue to do so long after the institution dies of its own weight. Prior to the existence of mass schooling in the United States, education happened. Historically, compulsory education has increased neither attendance nor literacy.[42] Literacy was not universal prior to compulsory education, and neither is it today. Literacy and education have long been values in our culture. We are more likely to cause youths to disvalue education by forcing them to attend school than by making education a market commodity.

The second assumption is more sticky; the belief is commonly held that society will somehow crumble if all children are not forced into school, that jobs will go unfilled, and progress will slow to an unacceptable rate. The truth is that long before public schools came onto the scene, there was human progress. In fact, the Industrial Revolution was hardly a product of mass public education, which became the norm only early in the twentieth century. In today's world, a high level of education is perceived as essential to basic survival, but the reality is that there remain endless means of making a living without a college degree. Many individuals learn enough by experience to manage a service station or restaurant, and others develop sophisticated, marketable computer skills by experimenting on the internet. Homeschooled individuals continue to outperform public school graduates in standardized tests, with average scores in

42. E. G. West, "Economic Analysis, Positive and Normative," in William F. Rickenbacker, ed. *The Twelve Year Sentence* (New York: Delta, Dell Publishing, 1974), pp. 163–91.

the 75th percentile rather than the 50th that public school tests reveal.[43] Highly successful individuals lacking college degrees may be exceptions to an accepted rule, but there is no evidence that society will fall to pieces without mass compulsory education.

Even if the above assumptions that compulsory education is essential to the functioning of society were true, tax credits and vouchers are not the solution. Although these schemes ostensibly seek to place schooling decisions back under parental control and open the educational system to market forces, the reality is quite different. In Pennsylvania there has existed for many years a system whereby private schools can use teacher resources, books, and curriculum materials just as public schools can. The catch, however, is that the private schools in Pennsylvania, whether or not they wish to avail themselves of these perks, must follow the same regulations as public schools regarding number of students per teacher, type of physical plant, number of school days, qualifications of teachers, and the like. Private schools in Pennsylvania are both more costly and more scarce than in states with less regulation of private schooling. In Florida, a bill to permit vouchers was recently passed. The new legislation offers vouchers only to students from poorly rated public schools and only if the private school receiving the voucher uses random selection procedures.[44] Obviously, this defeats the purpose of allowing the market to fix what is wrong with public schooling. Both of these examples clearly point out the fatal flaw in the voucher/tax credit argument: Once government has collected funds, they become government funds, and the redistribution follows government rules. Thus, vouchers and credits will not create a freer marketplace in education, or the competition needed to force the public schools to rise to the demands of consumers. Indeed, tax credits and vouchers

---

43. Brian D. Ray, "Fact Sheet 1" (Salem, Ore.: National Home Education Research Foundation, June 1997).
44. Florida State Legislature, *House Bill 751, Senate Bill 1756*, 1999.

threaten to destroy competition and entrench the public schools more deeply.

Schooling versus Education

The ultimate goal of public schooling is not the education of minds— training in problem-solving, research methods, logic, creativity, and critical thinking. These are skills easily acquired by children, who are developmentally driven to grow in skill and knowledge. On the contrary, in today's public schools, the real goal is equalization, homogenization, socialization. When children are poured en masse into buildings, placed in age-based groups, kept there for six hours a day, and given exactly the same things to do, education is not the result, homogenization is. Real education is rather an individual endeavor, in which children are challenged to think and understand, to expand their knowledge, to rise to their highest potential as individuals.

All children are not created the same, though they are indeed supposed to be equal under the law. Equal, however, does not mean that all children should have twelve years of schooling, that all children can and should learn algebra, that all children can and should read at age six. Equal means that given legal equality, all children have the right not to be prevented from reaching their full potential, whatever that may be. They have the right to explore themselves and strive for the best within themselves, to seek an eventual place in the world that fits their abilites and interests. And they have the right to be angry when they are prevented from achieving these goals. There is no corollary right to be given a costly tax-supported education on the false premise that all children can and should learn the same things at the same time. It is for parents and children to determine what the educational needs of a given child are and how best to meet these, whether in a large school, a small school, or a more informal setting.

As this is being written in mid-1999, public outcry rings continually about the tragedy at Columbine High School in Littleton, Colorado, in which fifteen individuals lost their lives; about the dramatic increase in school violence. The outcry is against guns and films and video games and trench coats. The reality is that a major cause of these tragedies as well as increased drug abuse and other destructive behaviors on the parts of teenagers is not the viewing of violent films or the availability of guns. It is alienation. Today's youth are alienated—from themselves and from society. Many experience a mismatch between the expected goal of school, to learn something and get ahead in life, and the reality, that learning is elusive, social control is ubiquitous, and the future, uncertain. Alienation manifests itself in different ways, but the spectrum of symptoms ranges from helplessness and despair to norm-violating behavior, rage and violence.[45]

Our children are unable to discover who they are and what they are and where they are going in life because there is a system in place with the power to *tell them*. They move without choice through twelve years of a process that bears no resemblance to the world they will then enter and gives little attention to their needs and goals as individuals. They have been stuck within a leviathan system with the ostensible goal of educating, but the true agenda of inculcating. In the United States, once the home of the free, the melting pot of nations, a refuge for individualism, a school system has become entrenched that belies the goal of the greatest nation on earth—that of educating people to think freely and try the untried. Sadly, the system does not know our children as unique individuals; it knows them only as public school students.

45. Margaret D. LeCompte and Anthony G. Dworkin, *Giving Up on School: Student Dropouts and Teacher Burnouts* (Newbury Park, Calif.: Corwin Press, 1991), p. 147.

BIBLIOGRAPHY

American Psychiatric Association, *Diagnostic and Statistical Manual of Mental Disorders*, Fourth Edition, Washington, D.C.: American Psychiatric Association, 1994.

Barkley, Russell A., *Attention Deficit Hyperactivity Disorder: A Handbook for Diagnosis and Treatment*, New York: Guilford Press, 1990.

Brown, B. Frank, *The Nongraded High School*, Englewood Cliffs, N.J.: Prentice-Hall, 1963.

Collins, Randall, *The Credential Society: An Historical Sociology of Education and Stratification*, Orlando, Fla.: Academic Press, 1979.

Dell, P. A., and Rose, F. David, "The impairing effect of environmental impoverishment in rats: A cognitive deficit?" IRCS Medical Science: *Psychology & Psychiatry* 14 (1986): 19–20.

Eberstadt, Mary, *Policy Review* 94 (April/May 1999).

Florida State Legislature House Bill 751, Senate Bill 1756, 1999.

"Glenbard West High School 1998 School Report Card," Glen Ellyn, Ill.: Glenbard Township District 87 Community Relations Office, October 1998.

Haskins, Ron, "Beyond Metaphor: The Efficacy of Early Childhood Education," *American Psychologist* 44 (1989): 274–82.

Hilmar, Nordvik, and Amponsah, Benjamin, "Gender differences in spatial abilities and spatial activity among university students in an egalitarian educational system," *Sex Roles* 38 (1998): 1009–23.

Hines, Melissa, Chiu, Lee, McAdams, Lou A., Bentler, Peter M., et al. "Cognition and the corpus callosum: Verbal fluency, visuospatial ability, and language lateralization related to midsagittal surface areas of callosal subregions," *Behavioral Neuroscience* 106 (1992): 3–14.

Japan Echo 25, no. 3 (June 1998).

Kaufman, Alan S., *Assessing Adolescent and Adult Intelligence*, Boston: Allyn & Bacon, 1990.

———, *Intelligent Testing with the WISC-R*, New York: John Wiley & Sons, 1979.

LeCompte, Diane, and Anthony G. Dworkin, *Giving Up on School: Student*

Dropouts and Teacher Burnouts, Newbury Park, Calif.: Corwin Press, 1991.

Linksman, Ricki, *How to Learn Anything Quickly*, Secaucus, N.J.: Carol Publishing, 1997.

Maccoby, Eleanor E., "Gender and Relationships," *American Psychologist* 43 (April, 1990): 513–520.

Montessori, Maria, *From Childhood to Adolescence*, New York: Schocken Books, 1973.

———, *The Discovery of the Child*, Madras, India: Kalakshetra Publications, 1948.

National Information Center for Children and Youth with Disabilities, "The education of children with special needs: What do the laws say?" *NICHCY New Digest Interim Update*, Washington D.C.: National Information Center for Children and Youth with Disabilities (October 1996).

Nesse, Randolph A., and Williams, George C., *Why We Get Sick: The New Science of Darwinian Medicine*, New York: Vintage Books, Random House, 1996.

Ray, Brian D., "Fact Sheet 1," Salem, Ore.: National Home Education Research Foundation, June 1997.

———, "Fact Sheet 2b," Salem, Ore.: National Home Education Research Institute, June 1997.

———, "Nationwide Study," Salem, Ore.: National Home Education Research Institute, June 1997.

Reite, Martin, Sheeder, Jeanelle, Teale, Peter, Richardson, M., Adams, Matthew, and Simon, Jack, "MEG based brain laterality: Sex differences in normal adults," *Neuropsychologia* 33 (1995): 1607–16.

Senior, Eileen M., "Learning disabled or merely mislabeled? The plight of the developmentally young child," *Childhood Education* 62 (1986): 161–65.

Sharan, Shlomo, "Cooperative Learning: A Perspective on Research and Practice," in Shlomo Sharan, ed., *Cooperative Learning: Theory and Research*, New York: Praeger, 1990, pp. 286–300.

Slavin, Robert E., "Comprehensive Cooperative Learning Models: Embedding Cooperative Learning in the Curriculum and the School," in Shlomo

Sharan, ed., *Cooperative Learning*, New York: Praeger, 1990, pp. 261–83.

Slavin, Robert E., Madden, Nancy A., Karweit, Nancy L., Dolan, Lawrence, Wasik, Barbara A., Shaw, Alta, Mainzer, K. Lynn, and Haxby, Barbara. "Neverstreaming: Prevention and early intervention as an alternative to special education," *Journal of Learning Disabilities* 24 (1991): 373–78.

Spring, Joel, *Education and the Rise of the Corporate State*, Boston: Beacon Press, 1972.

Sowell, Thomas, *The Vision of the Anointed*, New York: Basic Books, 1995.

Stevenson, Harold W., and James W. Stigler, *The Learning Gap*, New York: Summit Books, 1992.

Sugimoto, Yoshio, *An Introduction to Japanese Society*, Cambridge, U.K.: Cambridge University, 1997, p. 112.

Suzuki, David, and Oiwa, Keibo, *The Japan We Never Knew*, Toronto, Canada: Stoddart, 1996, pp. 289–303.

West, E. G., "Economic Analysis, Positive and Normative," in William F. Rickenbacker, ed., *The Twelve Year Sentence*, New York: Delta, Dell Publishing, 1974, p. 163–91.

Whitworth, Molly R., and Southwick, Charles H., "Sex differences in the ontogeny of social behavior in pikas: Possible relationships to dispersal and territoriality," *Behavioral Ecology and Sociobiology* 15 (1984): 175–82.

Woronoff, Jon, *The Japanese Social Crisis*, New York: St. Martin's, 1997, pp. 215–23.

CHAPTER FOUR

Individuality, Education, and Entrepreneurship

Sheldon Richman

INDIVIDUALS DIFFER dramatically one from another. At one level this fact is obvious, so commonplace that we all but lose our awareness and appreciation of it. At another level this truth is anything but obvious: It's startling. Individuals differ in ways that most people never imagine.

These differences have monumental implications for a host of important issues, particularly issues of public policy in a welfare state. Among the most important is education. Given the undeniable variation among individuals, what educational arrangement might best assure that they attain their intellectual potential? For more than 150 years, government in the United States has assumed responsibility for educating most children. Over the past several decades there has been a growing sense that it has been deficient in this role, prompting increasing numbers of parents to seek alternatives. Much of this failure can be traced to government's nature as a bureaucracy, which intrinsically limits its ability to provide individualized services. An educational system that is unable to cater to the inborn diversity among children is arguably worse than no educational system at all.

If that is so, the search for an alternative to government's virtual educational monopoly is all the more urgent. The tragedy of having children languishing in a "one size fits all" school system cannot be overstated.

But what would that alternative be? I contend that in place of bureaucracy we must have entrepreneurship in the provision of education services. Entrepreneurship, unlike bureaucracy, is best suited for the kind of world in which we live, a world not only of diverse individuals who require liberty to flourish, but also a world of uncertainty in which discovery of the unimagined is critical to our well-being.

To get the most out of entrepreneurship in education, full separation of school and state is required. Under separation, government would abandon the education business entirely and free parents and entrepreneurs to find the best ways to satisfy educational needs. This is admittedly a radical proposal with far-reaching implications. Government would not operate schools, allocate tax money to schools or parents, set standards, write curricula, certify teachers, govern admissions policy, or compel attendance. Only an open-ended entrepreneurial process will permit an uninhibited search for the best ways to face highly individualized educational challenges.

That process requires a particular institutional setting characterized by private property and free exchange. Anyone should be free to offer any service to potential customers, who are also free to accept or reject those services as they see fit. (The laws concerning misrepresentation and fraud would apply, of course.) We should not anticipate an educational process free of error. On the contrary, trial and error would provide a major advantage over the current system. The result will be an undreamed-of, open-ended array of services tailored to unique children, in place of the procrustean system administered by state, local, and, increasingly, federal bureaucracies.

INDIVIDUALITY

All human beings share the fundamental characteristics of (potential) rationality and volitional consciousness, as well as anatomical and other similarities, but every attribute is subject to wide variation. Common physical characteristics can—and do—differ vastly. Some differences are well known. Each person's fingerprints and DNA are unique. We readily perceive external physical differences among people. Human beings come in a variety of heights, shapes, colors, and weights. Eyes, ears, noses, mouths, arms, legs, hands, and feet range greatly in size. Skin tones vary from pale to dark. Hair differs in color, quality, and quantity. No two people look exactly alike, even "identical" twins.

Internally, the differences are just as pronounced, if not more so. Biochemist Roger J. Williams writes:

> [O]n our arrival as newborn babes each of us brings along a host of highly distinctive inborn characteristics. . . . [E]ach of us is built in a *highly distinctive way* in every particular . . . The basic answer to the question "Why are you an individual?" is that your body in every detail, including your entire nervous system and your brain (thinking apparatus), is highly distinctive.[1]

According to Williams, every organ in the human body is subject to the widest variation in size and shape. No two stomachs, livers, hearts, or brains are alike. Indeed, the differences between individual human brains are as pronounced as the differences between the brains of different species.[2] "Physiological individuality is exhibited to a marked degree no matter what area we consider," Williams continues. "In that of the senses, for example—seeing, hearing, tasting, smelling, the sense of touch, etc.—striking evidence of individ-

---

1. Roger J. Williams, *You Are Extraordinary* (New York: Random House, 1967), pp. 5, 9, 51. Emphasis in original.
2. Ibid., p. 7. Williams's picture of human differences is further confirmed by the reports about Albert Einstein's brain. See Lawrence K. Altman, "Key to Intellect May Lie in Folds of Einstein's Brain," *New York Times*, June 18, 1999.

uality can be found wherever we look."[3] Moreover, "Every newborn baby has a distinctive and complex pattern of inborn mental capacities. Each item in this pattern is derived from his human forebears, but the pattern with its interaction is unique."[4]

Nonphysical attributes have the same variety as physical features. People are different in myriad ways: sense of humor, talent, ambition, energy, mental quickness, sympathy, intelligence, interests, tastes, articulateness, facility with numbers and language, and so on.

We need not explore how many of these differences are accounted for by genetics and physiology and how many by environment. If people enter the world with individualized equipment, no two of them are *ever* in the identical environment. Any influences from their surroundings would be filtered through their inborn attributes. This interaction of nature and nurture might make a search for the proportional contribution of each not only futile but conceptually nonsensical.[5]

At any rate, what makes a person who he is can be accounted for to some extent by inborn physical differences. This is not to deny free will or volition in the some operations of consciousness. It is only to acknowledge that choice takes place within a particular context.

Human inequality has long created discomfort in some quarters. It has even been denied outright. In the entry on "Behaviorism" in the *Encyclopedia of the Social Sciences*, H. Kallen wrote that "at birth

3. Roger J. Williams, "Individuality and Its Significance in Human Life," in Felix Morley, ed., *Essays in Individuality* (Philadelphia: University of Pennsylvania Press, 1958), p. 131.

4. Roger J. Williams, *Free and Unequal: The Biological Basis of Individual Liberty* (1953; Indianapolis: Liberty Press, 1979), p. 100.

5. See H. George Resch, "Human Variation and Individuality," in William F. Rickenbacker, ed., *The Twelve-Year Sentence: Radical Views of Compulsory Schooling* (LaSalle, Ill.: Open Court, 1974), pp. 35–58.

human infants, regardless of their heredity, are as equal as Fords."[6] Discomfort over inequality has stemmed in part from the mistaken belief that human variation somehow might negate the principle of equality before the law. One is hard-pressed to see how that conclusion can be reached. The rule of law derives from man's ability to regulate his conduct and his need of liberty to live a truly human life. The principle is unaffected by human variation.

Another motive for denying inborn differences is the desire to indict a particular social-economic system for the inevitable differences in incomes. If the varying capacities of individuals can be ruled out as causes, then income differences can be attributed to social injustice.[7] This is simply the use of bad science to promote a political or economic agenda.

No effort to deny individual differences has succeeded in creating equality. Moreover, any social system premised on human interchangeability would court disaster. Variation is a law of nature, and nature, to be commanded, must be obeyed. We have little choice but to accept human inequality across the range of attributes. We can go further and suggest that these differences ought to be embraced with gusto and not merely accepted in the spirit of resignation. Individuation is the glory of mankind.[8]

To see this, imagine if every person were a carbon copy of every other. Life would indeed be bleak. More than that, it would be

---

6. Quoted in Ludwig von Mises, "On Equality and Inequality," *Modern Age* V (Spring 1961); reprinted in George A. Panichas, ed., *Modern Age: The First Twenty-Five Years* (Indianapolis: Liberty Press, 1988), p. 94.

7. On this point and others, see the sadly unappreciated essay by P. T. Bauer, "The Grail of Equality," in his *Equality, The Third World and Economic Delusion* (Cambridge, Mass.: Harvard University Press, 1981), pp. 8–25.

8. It is curious that political correctness demands the "celebration" of benign group differences while essentially denying individual differences. Group differences that may be liabilities in particular circumstances are also denied. Thus, feminist groups favor laws prohibiting fire departments from discriminating against women even though most women cannot pass the physical tests men can pass.

impoverished. It is the differences among individuals that account for advancement in life. "The development of individual variety tends to be both the cause and the effect of the progress of civilization," wrote Murray Rothbard.[9]

It is the differences among individuals that enable an elaborate division of labor to flourish in freedom. Under the division of labor, people with a variety of talents and interests specialize in what they do best, then trade the fruits of their labor with others. This enables each to be better off than he would be in the absence of inequality and specialization. "As civilization progresses," wrote Rothbard, "there is increasing opportunity for the greater development of each person's interests, talents, and reasoning in an expanding number of fields, leading to the growth of his human faculties."[10] Thus human diversity leads to specialization, which in turn leads to greater diversity and greater specialization in a never-ending process.[11] The spontaneous progress of mankind is toward greater individuation, yet greater cooperation (trade) as well. Consequently, "all despotisms," wrote Herbert Spencer, "whether political or religious, whether of sex, of caste, or of custom, may be generalized as limitations on individuality, which it is in the nature of civilization to remove."[12]

In freedom human beings become less alike. Under tyranny, they are forced to become more alike. Thus, as Rothbard put it, "Enthusiasm for equality should actually be viewed as anti-human. It tends to repress the flowering of individual personality and diversity, and, indeed, of civilization itself."[13] This is so because attempts to make people alike usually take the form of handicapping those with supe-

9. Murray N. Rothbard, *Education, Free and Compulsory* (Wichita, Kans.: Center for Independent Education, undated), p. 5.

10. Ibid.

11. Ludwig von Mises, *Socialism* (London: Jonathan Cape, 1936), pp. 292–95.

12. Herbert Spencer, *Social Statics* (New York: Robert Schalkenbach Foundation, 1970), p. 390.

13. Rothbard, *Education, Free and Compulsory*, p. 6.

rior ability to create.[14] Consistently applied, the doctrine of egalitarianism would cause society to atrophy and reduce mankind to primitivism.[15] As Rothbard noted, fictional descriptions of egalitarian societies are almost always horror stories, and for good reason. The conception of human society as an anthill is understandably terrifying.[16]

Inequality, therefore, is both an intractable fact and the key to human progress. (We shouldn't be surprised that respecting reality is a minimum requirement of success in any enterprise.) As classical liberal writers have long noted, there is but one sense of human equality that is valid: equality in freedom, or equality in natural rights. We may also call this equality before the law. This simply is the notion that all individuals, regardless of their differences, have a right to be free from aggressive force inflicted by others, whether through government or otherwise. In this condition, each person is able to attempt to develop to the fullest extent whatever abilities he has.

EDUCATION

Once the fact of individual diversity is established, it is only appropriate that education should take it into account. If adults differ significantly in inborn ways, then children do as well—and this undoubtedly has implications for their capacity to learn. Biochemical

---

14. Kurt Vonnegut Jr.'s short story "Harrison Bergeron," depicting a world in which the most able and intelligent are reduced to the level of the mediocre, illustrates the logic of egalitarianism. See Kurt Vonnegut Jr., *Welcome to the Monkey House* (New York: Dell Publishing Co., 1970).

15. See Murray N. Rothbard, *Egalitarianism as a Revolt against Nature and Other Essays* (Washington, D.C.: Libertarian Review Press, 1974), pp. 1–13. On the connection between equality and primitivism, also see Murray N. Rothbard, "Freedom, Inequality, Primitivism, and the Division of Labor," reprinted in Kenneth S. Templeton Jr., *The Politicization of Society* (Indianapolis: Liberty Press, 1979), pp. 85–126.

16. Rothbard, *Egalitarianism as a Revolt against Nature*, p. 5.

and psychological variation should be expected to create differences in how and at what pace individual children acquire knowledge and what they ought to attempt to learn. Most of what has passed for education has ignored this proposition.

The modern history of education appears to be based on the behaviorist premise that children are as equal as Fords. The education profession appears to acknowledge human variation, but appearances can be deceiving. As Roger Williams writes:

> Thus in the midst of lip service paid to individualism, many affairs of our daily lives are conducted as if human differences were only minor decorations on the cake, not to be seriously considered in the "realistic" business of life. True realism, however, would heed the individual differences, needs, and desires of human beings, recognizing the fact that frustrations, discontents, breakdowns, and even wars may arise out of their neglect.[17]

The modern history of education is largely a history of the failure to heed those differences. It is the story of government efforts to construct what historian David Tyack called the "one best system."[18] In that system, virtually all children start school at the same age, and spend the same number of hours a day, days a year, and years in school. Children the same age study essentially the same things on the same day, and are subjected to the same teaching methods. The system has not changed in its essence since it was devised.

Bruce Goldberg has shown that the development of "education theory" has been a series of episodes in which psychologists and others, working from the premise that all children are essentially alike, have claimed to have discovered a scientifically based universal

17. Williams, *Free and Unequal*, pp. 33–34.
18. David B. Tyack, *The One Best System: A History of American Urban Education* (Cambridge, Mass.: Harvard University Press, 1974).

method of schooling.[19] Depending on the theorist, the "science" used to determine how all children's minds develop has varied. Horace Mann, father of the American "common school" and among the first to proclaim the one right way to educate children, based his method on phrenology, the since-abandoned belief that bumps on the skull are intellectually and psychologically significant. Mann insisted that without that scientific foundation no one "should attempt to manage and direct . . . a child's soul."[20] His biographer wrote that Mann believed that "all children everywhere were essentially the same." Therefore, "all could be taught, once the correct techniques were determined."[21]

Later, the behaviorist John B. Watson and psychologist Jean Piaget made similar claims for their educational theories. Yet they failed to come up with a valid universal theory of education. Rather, on close examination, their views are revealed as arbitrary personal preferences dressed up in scientific language and imposed on children in an authoritarian manner. This is how children came to be force-fed progressivism, the "new math" and other so-called structuralism, and a host of other pretentious and failed approaches. "There is no such thing as educational science," Goldberg concludes.[22]

Yet parents are assured to this day that education experts have designed a scientific curriculum appropriate to all children. If children don't do well, then it must be their fault, not the fault of the experts. But, write David and Micki Colfax:

> The public school curriculum—which includes, at least theoretically, what is to be learned and when—is in fact nothing more than a hodgepodge of materials and assumptions resulting from the historical

19. Bruce Goldberg, *Why Schools Fail* (Washington, D.C.: Cato Institute, 1996).
20. Quoted in ibid., p. 5.
21. Quoted in ibid., p. 105.
22. Ibid., p. 102.

interplay of educational theories, political expedience, education fads and fashions, pretensions to culture, demagoguery, and demography. It is by no means, as professional educators would have it, a coherent "course of study" or, as the more pretentious among them would have it, a "distillation of our common culture."[23]

An eerie theme runs through the thinking of most educational theorists: That children begin as homogeneous pieces of raw material and are to be molded into a preconceived model of human being and good citizen. The denial that unique children have within them the principle of spontaneous growth (in the Aristotelian, not Rousseauian, sense), which requires loving guidance but not the potter's hand, is characteristic of architects of comprehensive school systems. In a typical statement of this premise, Horace Mann proclaimed, "Children are wax." Likewise, the sociologist Edward Ross declared that children were "little plastic lumps of dough" to be "shaped on the social kneadingboard." It is no coincidence that they also regarded children ultimately as property of the state.

This attitude is a key to understanding the public school culture and to distinguishing it from what would prevail if education were provided in a free market. Instead of schooling's being seen as a service offered to competent buyers (parents) in the marketplace, it has been regarded rather as the missionary or therapeutic work of an enlightened elite mercifully bestowed on the benighted and unappreciative masses. As Mann himself said, "We who are engaged in the sacred cause of education are entitled to look upon all parents as having given hostages to our cause." This public school culture, which sees children as empty vessels to be filled or, as one observer put it, sausages to be packed, was unlikely to aim for anything but conformity. Individuality was not something school activists were likely to be attuned to; if nothing else, it would complicate their mission.

23. Quoted in ibid., p. 103.

The use of the term "force-fed" above is appropriate because government began controlling education in the United States in the late 1830s. The progression of educational methods mentioned above came to pass in the context of compulsory state education. The history of educational "reform" was shaped by the institution that carried out the reforms. What are the essential characteristics of that institution?

Ever since comprehensive government control of American education began in Massachusetts and spread throughout the states in the subsequent half-century, it has been characterized by compulsion, first in financing and then in attendance. Whereas private schooling, which was found in abundance before the advent of "public education," required parents to pay fees (or to find a willing philanthropist to do so), government schools from their beginning were financed by taxation. This disassociation of service from payment made education appear free. It was often referred to as such. Government schools were free only in the sense that parents faced no marginal cost in sending their children there. That is only to say, however, that parents paid whether their children attended or not. (Taxpayers without children also paid.)

This form of financing has had two important consequences: First, it put fee-charging private schools at a disadvantage, and many of them went out of business in the early days. We might say that the government engaged in predatory pricing. Second, since education appeared free, parents were tempted to treat it as such. In other words, relieved of the need to sacrifice on behalf of their children's schooling, education could be taken for granted. Both consequences shifted oversight of education to government and related institutions and interests, such as schools of education and, later, teachers' unions.

The result was bureaucracy. Bureaucracy is the form of organization that obtains its revenues from other than willing buyers (or donors). Taxes are due regardless of how dissatisfied a citizen is with government services. Regardless of what other recourse he may have (for example, at the ballot box or by moving to another jurisdiction), he may not simply decline to pay and choose to hire the services of a competitor.

The word "bureaucracy" is often a pejorative, and for good reason. Bureaucracies are stereotypically self-serving organizations unresponsive to their ostensible "customers." Stereotypes usually have some basis. Considering that a bureaucracy has a guaranteed source of revenue and a more or less captive audience, responsiveness to those it theoretically serves is not to be expected. Human beings tend to economize on effort as in everything else. If the money comes in whether one's customers are satisfied or not, little effort will be expended in satisfying them.

Government schools and school districts are bureaucracies like any other government agencies. They began small and decentralized, moderating some of the malign features of bureaucracy, but over the years they have done what the public choice school of political economy would lead us to expect: They have grown larger and more centralized. With this tendency, the flaws of bureaucracy have become more aggravated.

The term "bureaucratic schools" has a particularly ugly ring to it. It summons up images of dreary buildings, inflexible procedures, and monotonous teachers all serving to force conformity on their charges. That has been the experience for millions of children. John Holt, who spent may years teaching, wrote:

> In these dull, ugly, and inhuman places, where nobody ever says anything either very true or truthful, where everybody is playing some kind of role, as in a charade, where the teachers are no more free to respond openly and honestly to the students than the students are free to respond to the teachers or each other, where the air practically vibrates with suspicions and anxiety, the child learns to live in a kind

of daze, saving his energies for those small parts of his life that are too trivial for the adults to bother with and thus remain his.[24]

Government schools have at least two reasons to favor conformity and thus to find education theories that assume uniformity convenient. First, a "one size fits all" service suits a bureaucracy's dynamics. A private firm has a clear test of success: the profit-loss statement. Managers can be instructed to make profit and the numbers will indicate if they have done so. A bureaucracy has no bottom line. Thus, its personnel cannot be put to the private sector's test. Rather, the bureaucracy will tend to generate myriad rules for its personnel to follow. The rules will foster conformity: All first-graders will do these letter and number exercises the fifth week of the semester; sixth-graders will read these books; eighth-graders will cover these math lessons; twelfth-graders will have the same science courses.

The second reason that government schools favor conformity is that they aspire to instill a particular notion of good citizenship in their students. From the government's perspective, good citizenship entails acquiescence and obeisance to authority. These are necessary in order to have taxes paid on time and regulations obeyed with minimum enforcement costs. Government counts on a good measure of "voluntary" compliance by its citizens, since the population always outnumbers the leaders and their enforcers. What better way to assure good citizenship than to drill it into young children in the government's own schools? This is why virtually all governments have aspired to control education. Teaching respect for political authority has spillover effects in the academic realm; it encourages an inappropriate deference to all authority and encourages an avoidance of independent thinking.

Observers have long criticized government schooling for its defiance of individuality. Wilhelm von Humboldt, the German liberal,

24. John Holt, *The Under-Achieving School* (New York: Delta, 1969), p. 28.

blamed state education for smothering individuality. He wrote in *The Limits of State Action* that "National education, since at least it presupposes selection and appointment of some particular instructor, must always promote a definite form of development, however careful to avoid such as error." Joseph Priestley wrote that "Instead, then, of endeavoring, by uniform and fixed systems of education, to keep mankind always the same, let us give free scope to everything which may bid fair for introducing more variety among us." In *On Liberty* John Stuart Mill wrote that "A general State education is a mere contrivance for molding people to be exactly like one another."

Herbert Spencer, in *Social Statics*, observed that the proposition that government must control education "is convertible into this—a government ought to mold children into good citizens, using its own discretion in settling what a good citizen is and how the child may be molded into one." Auberon Herbert, the English libertarian, complained that government schools, despite an appearance of localism, "must use the same class of teachers; they must submit to the same inspectors; the children must be prepared for the same examination, and pass in the same standards." And in the first *Mencken Chrestomathy*, H. L. Mencken wrote that:

> the teaching process, as commonly observed, has nothing to do with the investigation and establishment of facts. . . . Its sole purpose is to cram the pupils, as rapidly and as painlessly as possible, with the largest conceivable outfit of current axioms, in all departments of human thought—to make the pupil a good citizen, which is to say, a citizen differing as little as possible, in positive knowledge and habits of mind, from all other citizens.

In our time, John Taylor Gatto, a former public school teacher who won the highest honors in his profession, observed, "The truth is that schools don't teach anything but how to obey orders. . . . Schools are intended to produce, through the application of formulas, formulaic human beings whose behavior can be predicted and controlled." Or, as John Holt put it, "If an enemy spy from outer space were planning to take over earth, and his strategy were to prepare mankind for this takeover by making men's children as stupid as possible, he could find no better way to do it than to require them, for many hours a day, to be still and quiet." Roger Williams, condemning the "educational assembly line," warned that "if we continue to assume that all 'normal' children are alike and teach them accordingly, we are contributing to the too-prevalent tendency toward regimentation which can make any people easy prey to dictatorship."

The relationship between educational bureaucracy and democracy is relevant here. For many people, "public schools" are nearly sacred because they are draped with the mantle of democracy. It is hardly suspected that democracy is one of the biggest problems with today's schools. Why is it a good thing that education is in the democratic arena? Most people would not want other important parts of their lives in that arena. They would oppose subjecting religion or diet to a popular vote. Parents expect to have the authority and responsibility of guiding their children in these matters and would resent having to comply with majority votes on how their children practice religion (if at all) or what they eat.

Why then is democratically administered education sacred? It has something to do with the idea that in a democratic society, all children should have the same education experience (hence "common school"), which, among other things, is aimed at creating good democratic citizens. We could as validly argue that in a democratic society it would be best for children to have a common religious and nutritional upbringing.

Democratic administration of schools reinforces the bureaucratic tendency to see children as interchangeable and to teach on the basis of conformity. The spirit of democratic equality tends to encourage the belief that all children are entitled to the same educational services. After all, the parents are taxpayers and the children are future citizens. Today we see efforts in states to equalize funding for school districts, including the elimination of the real estate tax as a source of financing because it leads to large disparities in public school budgets. It is increasingly regarded as unjust for some school districts to have more money than others.

Democratic control, moreover, necessarily translates into control by, at best, weakly accountable "experts" whose educational pseudoscience leads them to operate on the basis of alleged universal laws of learning. Nothing has been more tempting to a social scientist than to mimic the hard sciences in an effort to bring respectability to his profession. As a result, children have been treated like guinea pigs, subjected to faddish experimentation devised in the schools of education and the departments of social psychology.

The shift to control by self-styled experts has several sources. Contrary to the civics textbooks, "the people" do not direct the democratic process. They vote for school board members and state and federal officials, but the process neither encourages nor permits real authority by citizens. Since each citizen has only one vote, his choice at the ballot box is undecisive and thus costless. That is, when a voter chooses a candidate, unlike when he chooses a breakfast cereal, he doesn't perforce get his choice and forgo the alternative. Toothless choosing such as this induces rational ignorance in voters. If your action cannot effectuate your preference, why go to the trouble of making an intelligent decision?

Rational ignorance leaves a vacuum, which politics like nature abhors. It is filled by relatively small, well-organized interest groups (teachers' unions, for instance) carrying out agendas that don't necessarily mesh with the interests of parents and children. The upshot is that schools will tend to be controlled by professional educationists, whose orientation will be to see children as lumps of clay awaiting molding.

This is not to say that government schools can never take individuality into account—only that they will be severely limited and even crippled in their ability to identify differences and to accommodate them. As a virtual monopoly, government schools cut themselves off from the vital discovery process that characterizes an entrepreneurial environment. State schools thus draw from a stagnant pool of "experts" operating under the perverse incentives generated by a system that gets it money by taking it from taxpayers rather than by satisfying willing customers. These deficiencies will become more clear as we contrast bureaucracy with entrepreneurship.

The schools' uniformity and demand for conformity are harmful to children, who require variety and individualized learning. Teachers report that students are bored, angered, and impeded from using initiative. They are kept busy with activities that seem to have that as their only objective. Following rules and satisfying an authority's arbitrary requirements have become the supreme end. Most students put up with it, the brightest ones learning how to use the system when necessary. Others suffer in silence, their natural curiosity snuffed out at an early age. Still others seek escapes, in cliques or perhaps in drugs and alcohol. Others may turn to violence, against self or others. We shouldn't underestimate what the denial of individuality can yield. In *Notes from the Underground*, Dostoyevsky's narrator says that:

> Man may purposely, consciously choose for himself even the harmful and the stupid, even the stupidest thing—just so that he will have the right to wish the stupidest thing, and not be bound by the duty to have only intelligent wishes. For this most stupid thing, this whim of ours, gentlemen, may really be more advantageous to us than anything on earth, especially in certain cases. In fact, it may be the most advantageous of all advantages even when it brings us obvious harm and contradicts the most sensible conclusions of our reason concerning our advantage. Because, at any rate, it preserves for us the most

important and most precious thing—our personality, our individual-ity.[25]

ENTREPRENEURSHIP

The alternative to bureaucratic control of schools is entrepreneurship. This form of administration is well suited to providing an individualized service such as education.

Before detailing the merits of entrepreneurship for education, let's look at the need for and nature of entrepreneurship per se. Entrepreneurship is the human race's answer to scarcity and ignorance. We live in a world where ends outnumber means. "Means" is used here in its widest sense, including time. Because there are many competing uses for scarce means, we all want to assure that more important ends are achieved before less important ones. In a large, complex society, this is not a clear-cut matter.[26]

Our ignorance complicates things. We can't know the future precisely or in its entirety. All action takes place in time, creating uncertainty and the risk of error. We can't be sure what will happen in the interval between the start of a course of action and its conclusion. This sort of ignorance is not rational, or chosen, ignorance. We choose to remain ignorant of many things because the benefits of dispelling that ignorance are not worth the costs. Another kind of ignorance is what economist Israel Kirzner calls "utter ignorance." It is an ignorance of which we are not aware and therefore we cannot deliberately

25. Quoted in Angus Crane, "The Day We Read No More," *The Freeman: Ideas on Liberty*, March 2000, p. 53. The school shootings of recent years are brought to mind by that passage.

26. The relative importance of ends is determined by individuals. Only individuals act to achieve values, and all action is intended to exchange a lesser preferred state of affairs for a more preferred state of affairs. Society does not act and cannot be said to have ends apart from those of its members. In discussing entrepreneurship, we must not lose sight of methodological individualism or this "subjectivism" of values, which is not to be confused with ethical subjectivism.

dispel; it is dispelled by unanticipated discovery and surprise—by serendipity.

Such ignorance and discovery are possible because the world, to use Kirzner's term, is open-ended. In a closed world, all means and ends are assumed to be known; we simply calculate the best paths to our chosen ends. In an open-ended world, by contrast, some means and ends are unknown. No matter how satisfied a person may be with a course of action, he can't be sure that he won't discover something tomorrow that he will wish he had known today. This fact creates the conditions for entrepreneurship.

All action is entrepreneurial; it seeks to replace the present situation with a better one in an uncertain future and thus entails the risk of failure and loss. Everyone, then, is an entrepreneur. Open-endedness creates the opportunity for *professional* entrepreneurs, people who seek money profits by being alert to hitherto overlooked opportunities that would make people better off if only they knew about them.

As Kirzner has elaborated, entrepreneurs in a market economy use signals provided by the price system to discover those opportunities. They do so by divining where resources are bringing a lower return than they otherwise might. For example, if a given combination of resources priced at $50 produces a good that sells for $60 but could produce another good that would sell for $75, an alert entrepreneur has a profit incentive to bid the resources away from the first use and to make the alternative product. If he anticipates consumers correctly, he earns a profit. It is as though he has turned $60 into $75. He has revealed hidden information about the use of resources for which the buyers of the new product will be grateful. (Producers of the old product will be encouraged to become more efficient or to find substitute resources.) If he is wrong and consumers are unwilling to pay more than $59, he loses.

The relevant point is that without the lure of profit, useful knowledge—about new goods and services, as well as new ways to make existing goods and services—would remain undiscovered, to the detriment of consumers. As Kirzner has put it, the possibility of profit stimulates alertness. Entrepreneurship is at the core of what F. A. Hayek called the market's "discovery procedure." Thus the entrepreneurial system benefits people generally, and not just those who make a profit.

The application of the principle of entrepreneurship to education is straightforward. The world is open-ended with respect to educational services. There is presumably much to be discovered about how children learn. We can't know in advance what there is to be discovered or who will discover it, yet this is important information. We should want to maximize the chance that such information will be uncovered and made available to the rest of us.

In a free education market, entrepreneurs will be lured by the prospect of profit to uncover new methods and objectives with respect to learning and teaching. The only limit on their search, ultimately, is the buyers of education services, who have the power to turn thumbs down on any offering.

An education environment dominated by government stifles that process. "Free" state schools artificially constrict the demand for nongovernment services, reducing the profit potential in this sector of the marketplace. Entrepreneurs naturally gravitate to where the potential returns are the greatest. This is not to say that no entrepreneurial activity occurs. As "Hooked on Phonics" and Sylvan Learning Centers show, the government's deficiencies create business opportunities—but the spectrum of opportunities is not as large as it would otherwise be.

The government's virtual monopoly is itself ill-suited to engage in entrepreneurial discovery. As pointed out, elected officials and bureaucrats, despite the best motives, do not have the incentive to find better ways of educating children. (The achievement of higher test scores is not to be mistaken for education.) Even if school-board members, principals, and teachers sincerely wanted to find better methods, they are in no position to engage in appropriate experimentation. Yet experimentation—trial and error—are important to discovery. Joseph Priestley observed that education is an art requiring "experiments and trials," "unbounded liberty, and even caprice." He added that "from new and seemingly irregular methods, perhaps something extraordinary and uncommonly great may spring."

Government school systems do engage in experimentation, but it an *inappropriate* kind in at least two respects. It is not checked by consumers' freedom of choice; compulsory schools *impose* experimentation on children. Moreover, when governments experiment, they risk committing errors that will effect thousands, even millions, of children over a long period. Several years ago the State of California confessed error and abandoned the whole-language method of teaching reading after a decade of subjecting millions of children to its mistake. By contrast, error in the marketplace tends to occur on a far smaller scale and for a shorter period of time. If parents chose and directly paid for their children's education, they would be unlikely to stay with a method that yielded results as poor as California's former reading instruction.

In a free education market, anyone with a new idea and a willingness to risk his capital would be at liberty to offer goods and services directly to parents. In a government school system, innovators have to persuade bureaucrats to add new ideas to the existing curriculum. Before embracing an idea, the bureaucrats would have to recognize its potential merit, but institutional forces work against that recognition. For example, out of bureaucratic inertia, administrators will tend to favor current programs, or they'll be reluctant to make changes that would offend vested interests, such as the teachers' unions.

The upshot is that while the marketplace puts no arbitrary barrier between an innovator and his potential customers, a politically based education system erects an all but impenetrable bureaucratic barrier whose function is to repel new ideas perceived as a threat to the status quo.

To be sure, an entrepreneur may be unable to offer an innovative service if he fails to raise capital. But that would mean only that no other entrepreneur saw the same potential in the idea. That economic barrier is different from the protectionist school board that stands in the way of a new idea. Moreover, there is only one school board in each district, but there usually is more than one source of capital. If necessary, an innovator can save up his own capital. No single authority has life-and-death power over his idea. Of course, an innovator turned down by one school board could try another school district, where he might succeed. That does the parents in the first district little good, however. Thus, competition among school districts, such as it exists, is of limited benefit to consumers of educational services.

The advantage of educational entrepreneurship over bureaucracy is clear. The only filter between innovators and buyers is the judgment of the commercial potential of new ideas—that is, the prospects for acceptance by parents.

This advantage means more than openness to new "big" ideas about instructional methods or school organization. Many important advancements are made as the result of small, accidental innovations. Educational bureaucracies overconcerned with rules are likely to discourage the pursuit of innovations stumbled on in the course of teaching. The rules tend to be paramount. Good teachers may defy the rule-makers, but they are unlikely to talk about it openly. Decentralized enterprises are more apt to encourage serendipity, or at least not stand in the way of it. If one school fails in this respect, a competitor won't.

In his work on the division of knowledge in society, F. A. Hayek emphasized the importance of knowledge that is unarticulated and scattered. In schools, teachers have skills in working with children (a form of knowledge) that can't be articulated. Unlike centralized bureaucracies, decentralized firms are more likely to capitalize on such knowledge. Competitive pressures will provide an incentive for market-based schools to encourage and use discoveries made by the people closest to the action.

The virtues of competition in other goods and services have been well documented. When parents are free to choose their children's schools and aren't required to pay for a system they don't use, schools will tend to be better and more responsive to individualized needs. Nothing focuses the proprietor's mind like the customers' freedom to go elsewhere. Can the profit motive be counted on to produce good service? Adam Smith long ago pointed out that the butcher, baker, and brewer nourish us not because they love us but because they love themselves. He went on to say that service in the market would not be nearly as good if the motive were altruism.

Critics of private education fear that parents won't be astute enough to recognize quality education. The criticism goes back to John Stuart Mill—but it is self-subverting. If most parents won't know a good school when they encounter one, how will they know a good candidate for school board? Parents know more than they are given credit for. Even if they don't, that would not be enough to make a fully private educational system unworkable. Most people don't know how an automobile engine or a furnace works, yet they manage to find competent service for those machines by relying on independent sources of information, including consumer guides, newspapers, and word-of-mouth referrals. The marketplace promotes a benign free-rider phenomenon. When merchants cater to knowledgeable consumers, they spare the rest of us the need to engage in exhaustive research. We free-ride off those with greater expertise and inclination to investigate.

The same thing would happen with education. Parents who felt unqualified to judge schools directly would rely on formal channels of information (books, magazines, web sites) and informal channels (friends and neighbors). The market's built-in consumer protection features are badly unappreciated. Institutions such as *Consumer*

Reports and Underwriters Laboratories are so familiar they are taken for granted, yet they provide protection that the government could never hope to equal. In any market, trust is a firm's most important asset. It will go to great lengths to garner and enhance it. The possibility of a fly-by-night outfit always exists, but a little vigilance goes a long away in avoiding them. The Internet has made avoidance even easier.

The temptation to dismiss the case for a free market in education as "just theory" should melt before the mountain of historical evidence illustrating that educational freedom works. From antiquity we find that where there was educational freedom there was educational excellence. In ancient Athens, writes Andrew Coulson, government did not run schools.

> Anyone who wished could open a school, setting whatever curriculum and tuition he deemed appropriate. From among the available teachers, parents were free to choose whichever one taught the things they wanted their children to learn, at a price they could afford. Since the schools were run as private enterprises, they had to compete to attract students, and this kept prices relatively low. Even the poorest families apparently sent their sons to school for a few years despite the absence of state funding. . . . Athenian parents had complete discretion over the content and manner of their children's education.[27]

Coulson points out that freedom and competition spurred Athenian educators to innovate. "Elementary schools altered their curricula to meet changing parental demands, and an entirely new educational institution, secondary schooling, was brought into being as a result of market forces."[28] The result? "By all accounts, Athens was the most literate society in the Western world at that time."[29] It was also

---

27. Andrew Coulson, *Market Education: The Unknown History* (New Brunswick, N.J.: Transaction Publishers, 1999), pp. 40, 49.

28. Ibid., p. 43.

29. Ibid., p. 47.

prosperous, scientifically advanced, culturally sophisticated, substantially free.

Likewise, the Islamic world from the late sixth to eleventh centuries was largely without government involvement in education. In Persia, market-based schools predate the birth of Mohammed in 570.

> Just as it had in Athens and republican Rome, schooling flourished under these circumstances [of little or no state intervention], and a fairly coherent education system evolved. Education generally reached even the poorest children thanks to the religious and secular grant-maintained schools, and to the profound conviction of the time that every child should achieve at least basic literacy and a knowledge of scripture.[30]

Again, the results were remarkable. Literacy, poetry, philosophy, mathematics, and the sciences blossomed. That era unfortunately came to an end in the mid-eleventh century, when government found the schools useful for inculcating political and religious doctrines. "What had been a vibrant and diverse intellectual society gradually began to calcify."[31]

The experience was similar in England, the American colonies, and the young American republic before the advent of "free" and compulsory schooling.[32] Economists Jack High and Jerome Ellig observe that "Private education was widely demanded in the late 18th and 19th centuries in Great Britain and America. The private supply of education was highly responsive to that demand, with the consequence that large numbers of children from all classes received sev-

30. Ibid., p. 62.
31. Ibid., p. 64.
32. See generally E. G. West, *Education and the State: A Study in Political Economy*, 3rd edition, revised and expanded (Indianapolis: Liberty Fund, 1994).

eral years of education."[33] European visitors, most famously Alexis de Tocqueville, found Americans to be literate and well-educated. Historian Robert Seybolt notes that competition drove the educational process: "In the hands of private schoolmasters the curriculum expanded rapidly. Their schools were commercial ventures, and, consequently, competition was keen. . . . Popular demands, and the element of competition, forced them not only to add new courses of instruction, but constantly to improve their methods and technique of instruction."[34]

Evidence of wide literacy is to be found in the thriving publishing industry in the colonies and young republic. The pamphlets of Thomas Paine, the novels of Sir Walter Scott and James Fenimore Cooper, and the *Spelling Book* of Noah Webster sold in that population the equivalent of tens of millions of copies. In 1828, the *Journal of Education* pointed out that

> For meeting the intellectual wants of this [population] of 12,000,000, we have about 600 newspapers and periodical journals. There is no country, (it is often said), where the means of intelligence are so generally enjoyed by all ranks and where knowledge is so generally diffused among the lower orders of the community, as in our own. . . . [W]ith us a newspaper is the daily fare of almost every meal in almost every family.[35]

Freedom and competition apparently permitted and encouraged widespread education. Did it encourage *individualized* education? Most likely the answer is yes. No authority promulgated educational

33. Jack High and Jerome Ellig, "The Private Supply of Education: Some Historical Evidence," in Tyler Cowen, ed., *The Theory of Market Failure* (Fairfax, Va.: George Mason University Press, 1998), pp. 378–79.

34. Quoted in ibid., p. 368.

35. Quoted in E. G. West, "The Spread of Education Before Compulsion: Britain and America in the Nineteenth Century," *The Freeman: Ideas on Liberty*, July 1996, p. 492.

standards applicable to everyone in its jurisdiction. Objectives were set by parents and children. Educational services were provided by many independent schools, which no doubt differed in their approaches to teaching. Many children were taught by tutors or parents and thus received individualized instruction. Education historian Lawrence Cremin observes:

> If one considers the 89 men who signed either the Declaration of Independence or the Constitution or both, it is clear that the group is a collective outcome of provincial education in all its richness and diversity. Of the 56 signers of the Declaration, 22 were products of provincial colleges, 2 had attended the academy conducted by Francis Alison at New London, Pennsylvania, and the others represented every conceivable combination of parental, church, apprenticeship, school, tutorial, and self-education, including some who studied abroad. Of the 33 signers of the Constitution, who had not also signed the Declaration, 14 were products of the provincial colleges, one was a product of the Newark Academy, and the remainder spanned the same wide range of alternatives.[36]

Did any two of them have the same education? It is unlikely.

The supply of individualized education depends on the demand. A private educator may offer instruction tailored to the student, but if parents want a traditional education for their children, that educator may go out of business. Since most parents are themselves products of public schools, they tend to believe the traditional assembly-line education is appropriate. Much of the school-reform movement aims to return to older teaching methods that ignored individuality. Individualists will have to create their own market.

Today we see signs of discontent with assembly-line education. Homeschooling, which is quintessentially individualized learning, is

---

36. Lawrence Cremin, *American Education: The Colonial Experience, 1607–1783* (New York: Harper & Row, 1970), p. 544; quoted in Samuel L. Blumenfeld, *Is Public Education Necessary?* (Boise, Idaho: The Paradigm Co., 1985), p. 20.

growing. The number of homeschoolers more than tripled in the 1990s and stands at over a million.[37] It has been spectacularly successful.[38] Alternative schools are also flourishing. Part of what fuels this growth is growing disenchantment with what one parent called the "one size fits all" model used by government schools. Another complained that "public schools have to be all things to all people, and I think many parents are starting to look for much more than that."

Still, almost 90 percent of children attend government schools, indicating a still small demand for individualized learning. Most private schools are not much better than public schools. Is that likely to change even if government were to leave education to the private sector? There is reason to think so. Bruce Goldberg suggests that educational freedom will stimulate an examination of the very premises of traditional education. "[A] system of competing schools will produce a vigorous and thorough discussion of standards," he writes.[39] An entrepreneurial system will bring competing standards, small-scale bold experimentation, and increasing attention to children's individuality. Some daring education entrepreneurs will offer individualized "schooling" for the small market that already exists for it. As this happens, more and more parents will encounter that approach, discuss it, investigate it and, before long, embrace it. When that happens, the number of providers will grow. Eventually, individualism may come to dominate the education market.

There is reason to doubt that the most popular education reforms—vouchers and charter schools—will move us in that direction. A charter school is a school authorized and funded by a local school district to fulfill an approved mission that presumably departs from

37. Rene Sanchez, "Popularity Grows for Alternatives to Public Schools," *Washington Post*, October 1, 1997, p. A1.

38. Jay Mathews, "A Home Run for Home Schooling; Movement Can Point to High Test Scores in National Study," *Washington Post*, March 24, 1999, p. A11

39. Goldberg, *Why Schools Fail*, p. 108.

the mission of other schools. The charter school is typically exempted from many of the rules enforced by the district, allowing it some measure of autonomy. A voucher plan permits parents to enroll their children in private schools, using government-financed vouchers to pay some or all of the tuition. Both reforms are intended to stimulate competition for the public schools.

The wish to provide parents with new school choices is praiseworthy, but the reforms suffer serious flaws. In both cases, government at some level would continue to pay for education. This has several important consequences. First, with financing comes conditions. It is unlikely that a system to transfer taxpayers' money to schools not directly under the authority of school boards will be approved without rules designed to assure accountability. The result will be illusory choice, since state-regulated schools will resemble state-operated schools.

In the case of charter schools, the rules are embodied in a school's government-approved charter, which sets out its mission. School boards have the power to reject and revoke charters and, presumably, to demand modifications. The autonomy is never complete.

In the case of vouchers, the issuing authority will almost surely have the power to impose conditions on schools for eligibility. There are many precedents for this. The federal government imposes obligations on colleges and universities that accept students with government loans and grants. In Wisconsin the state Supreme Court has ruled that vouchers do not violate the separation of church and state so long as religious schools allow students to opt out of the sectarian parts of the curriculum. That restriction would exclude from the program any school that integrates religion throughout its course of study. The new Florida voucher plan includes requirements with which private schools must comply in order to participate. European nations have long used government funding to regulate private religious schools.

Another consequence of government funding is that it preserves the most pernicious feature of state control: parental irresponsibility. If parents do not consciously and directly pay for, as well as select, their children's education, they will tend to be complacent. Giving up something of value in order to educate one's child produces a sense of responsibility in many private school parents that is sadly lacking in public school parents, who see education as free. This may be the main reason why homeschooling and private schools get better results.[40] Vouchers and charter schools do not restore financial responsibility to parents.

After surveying the history of education, Andrew Coulson concluded that four elements correlate with success: freedom and competition on the supply side, and choice and *financial responsibility* on the demand side.[41] In other words, the way to foster worthwhile education, which will sooner or later be understood to mean individualized education, is to give parents full responsibility for their children.

We shouldn't be surprised that financial responsibility is a critical component. Without it, entrepreneurship cannot be complete, since parents' opportunity costs are distorted by state funding; their choices will be affected the funding mechanism.

A fully entrepreneurial educational process requires the complete separation of school and state. Government should have no role, aside from enforcing contracts. It should not even require parents to minimally educate their children or compel school attendance, because those seemingly benign edicts would permit the state to define "education," "school," and other terms. Definition is destiny. Once government controls the definitions it controls education. We'll be back to where we started: insipid schooling, bored children, ignored and stifled individuality.

40. See Marshall Fritz, "A Better Brand of Parent," *The Freeman: Ideas on Liberty*, September 1999, pp. 8–11.

41. Coulson, *Market Education*, p. 306.

INDEX

PHILOSOPHIC REFLECTIONS
ON A FREE SOCIETY

Business Ethics in the Global Market
Tibor R. Machan, editor

Education in a Free Society
Tibor R. Machan, editor

Morality and Work
Tibor R. Machan, editor